Servants in the
House of the Masters

Servants in the House of the Masters

◆

A social class primer for educators, helping professionals, and others who want to change the world

Signe M. Kastberg, Ph.D.

iUniverse, Inc.
New York Lincoln Shanghai

Servants in the House of the Masters

A social class primer for educators, helping professionals, and others who want to change the world

iUniverse books may be ordered through booksellers or by contacting:

iUniverse
2021 Pine Lake Road, Suite 100
Lincoln, NE 68512
www.iuniverse.com
1-800-Authors (1-800-288-4677)

Because of the dynamic nature of the Internet, any Web addresses or links contained in this book may have changed since publication and may no longer be valid.

The views expressed in this work are solely those of the author and do not necessarily reflect the views of the publisher, and the publisher hereby disclaims any responsibility for them.

ISBN: 978-0-595-46942-0 (pbk)
ISBN: 978-0-595-91226-1 (ebk)

Printed in the United States of America

for my parents,
Orla and Bertha Kastberg,
who provided constant love and support
and by their example,
the inspiration to be my own person
and to persevere despite the obstacles.

Contents

Acknowledgements

Many people participated in the development of this book. First and foremost, thanks go to the individuals whose voices reverberate throughout these pages; the women and men who agreed to allow you to read about their experiences and how those experiences shaped their lives. A number of persons with expertise in social class issues read prior drafts of the manuscript and it is no doubt vastly improved due to their suggestions: Anthony Potts, Jake Ryan, Judith Howard, Irvin Peckham, David Hursh, and Allison Hurst. My dissertation chair, later department chair, and now friend and colleague, Lisa Lopez Levers, provided much needed guidance and knowledgeable support throughout the initial research and writing process. The University of Rochester awarded funding for a portion of the travel required for my initial research, which was greatly appreciated.

I am indebted to Darlene Miller, who was the first person to join with me in believing that social class issues merited further exploration, especially as they played out in higher education. This provided the impetus for my dissertation research. Likewise, the friendly voices of the Working-Class Academics group helped keep me going through the research and writing phases of my study.

Thanks to my hometown friends, who have witnessed my departure from home both literally and figuratively, but chose to remain my friends despite the geographic and social distance. Sueann, Lauretta, Nancy, and other Schuylerville friends, you're the best!

Finally, I am most deeply grateful to my family, who saw me suffer through many iterations of the book and hours of divided attention as I worked towards its publication. Special thanks to Max and Chloe for hanging in there through the tough times.

PART I

Introduction and Overview

Introduction:
Who Cares About Class?

In 1921, an immigrant arrived in the United States from Denmark, not able to speak English. This young man left his country due to the common practice of early testing which determined one's future options for education and vocation. At age 14, his test-selected career was not to his liking; therefore, he quit school and became a baker's apprentice. Upon arriving in the United States, he learned English on the streets and began work in the kitchens of New York City, later taking seasonal work in the summer resort town of Lake George, New York.

Half a world away from Denmark, a 15-year-old girl dropped out of school in upstate New York for quite another reason: she had only two dresses to wear; one for church and the other for the remaining six days of the week. She feared the ridicule of her peers based on her attire, so she went to work as a laborer in a textile factory and lived in a boarding house. From there, she turned to waitressing for better wages.

This unlikely couple met and married, doing seasonal work in Florida, Nantucket, and the Adirondacks. When their first child was born, they settled in New York State due to their belief that it had the best educational opportunities, and they believed that education would be "the way out" for their child. They built a one-room house on a dirt road on 20 acres of swampland, and the young mother stayed home with their child.

A second child came along by surprise, as did the next two. They added a room onto the house as each child was born. Indoor plumbing was installed after the second child was born; prior to this they used an outhouse and water pump, walking through the deep snow and cold in winter.

When I, the fourth child, came along, my hard-working mother was in her 40's and my father in his 50's. I was raised with the conflicting knowledge that I was not wanted, but was loved. My parents were busy, too busy for me. With inadequate health care and the constant strain of living on the edge financially, they grew old and tired far too soon.

My father worked long hours, especially in the summer when "the season" was busy, so the family didn't see him much. He worked in a hot restaurant kitchen in the

3

summer's 90-degree heat from 10 in the morning 'til 10 at night, six days a week, making very little money. My mother was always busy with cleaning, cooking, and all the duties required to care for four children and manage a household budget based on poverty wages. There was often not enough water for bathing and laundry, as the well sometimes ran dry. One inch of water in the tub was allowed for baths. There was no shower. There was no dryer, and the old washer required that the clothes be manually wrung out after washing.

We children played in the woods and swamp, blissfully ignorant of the fact that this place would be considered a tar-paper shack by others. My mother was ashamed of our house and did not invite anyone over, contributing to a fairly isolated existence.

I started school at age four, not "ready" cognitively nor socially, but because my mother was more than ready for me to go to school. I began what would be a successful school experience, based not on the creativity or stimulation of the school, which was entirely lacking in a rural working-class institution, but on native intelligence and resourcefulness. My mother made sure all her children had plenty of clothes to wear, sewing them herself and—over time—teaching her daughters to sew as well.

Our family went to the library every week, where I always left with a stack of books that I read voraciously. Everyone in the family enjoyed reading, and books were all around the house. My father also enjoyed classical music, and played these records on a cheap Montgomery Wards record player so we children would learn to appreciate this music, occasionally quizzing us on the composers.

In fifth grade I received an award for having the highest academic average in my class. At home, there were squirrels running across the ceiling and gnawing holes into the rooms below; there were snakes living in the basement, where it was cool in summer and warm in winter. A cow visited to graze in the starlight under my bedroom window, and a horse regularly visited the birdfeeder in the day. The house was increasingly shabby and worn with the tracks of many feet and no money to repair a leaking roof or cracks in the foundation. The interior walls had never been painted; the original sheetrock was spattered with the spray of warm soda bottles being opened at the wrong time and in the wrong place.

In seventh grade I was placed in one of the highest tracks. By then I had learned to sew my own clothes for school, and my mother returned to work part-time at a farm stand selling apples and plants to rural and seasonal customers. In the upper tracks students took a foreign language in grades seven and eight; however, we were then required to re-take it at the same level in ninth grade due to the school's inability to accommodate any changes to their traditional step-wise structure.

In preparation for ninth grade, I was encouraged by my guidance counselor to take typing and shorthand; my parents didn't argue. They respected authority, and had no higher aspiration for me other than that I get married so I would be "taken care of." If I had to work, hopefully I would get a "sit down" job so I didn't have to be on my feet all day as they did.

I didn't think about going to college, although my siblings had gone and my parents had told me that I could go. In addition, no teacher or counselor at school even mentioned the idea of college to me, despite my excellence in academics. In April of my senior year, basically for lack of any idea of what else to do, I applied to the college and program where my sister had gone—what was then called "nursery education" (now early childhood development) at a two-year state school.

At high school graduation I received awards for excellence in business subjects. I received grants, loans and a work-study award to attend college, and majored in secretarial science. My academic talents were noticed by one professor, and he encouraged me to go on for more education. I transferred as a junior to Skidmore College, and majored first in English education (to become a teacher) and then when I found I had lost some credits in transferring from the state school, I switched to English literature so as to be able to graduate in four years, continuing to work part-time. Extending my stay in college for even one additional semester did not seem to be a viable option due to financial limitations.

It was at Skidmore that I first clearly saw social class distinctions—wealthy young women dressed in Saks Fifth Avenue as opposed to my jeans and sweatshirts. Most other students did not work while they studied as I did. I felt a profound sense of not belonging socially and in the classroom as well, where many students came from elite private schools and international travel experiences. One faculty member told me that what I thought actually mattered—a precious gift! However, she did not get tenure and was soon gone.

Without career guidance, upon graduation I took the first job I applied for and was offered, as a secretary at Skidmore College. I typed papers for students to keep afloat financially, scraping by on a tiny salary, paying student loans, apartment rent, and car payments; often eating rice and eggs for dinner, counting pennies until the next pay day. It was during these years that I discovered myself as an intelligent person, capable of more. I continued taking courses in various fields with free tuition for employees. When the Skidmore secretaries began agitating for higher wages, one faculty member commented that "the secretaries should learn to manage their money better." When he learned that these tiny salaries were at the poverty level, he publicly apologized. I knew I had to move on, just to survive.

I got a lucky break with some help from workplace friends and got my first professional position as an academic advisor and financial aid officer at another institution. Here I was accepted as a professional, not looked down upon as an outsider or someone who doesn't belong. After a short time, I realized that I couldn't move up in that orga-nization without a master's degree. I began studies at SUNY Albany, attending class at night after a full day of work, but then my imagination prodded me against my own beliefs about who I was and where I belonged, and I applied to Harvard Univer-sity, almost as a "dare" to myself.

I sold my only possession, a worn out car, and went to Harvard with a scholarship and loans, fearful of failure but ready to prove that I was equal to the challenge. I worked hard at my academics, worked part-time at work-study jobs while a full-time graduate student, and typed papers until 2:00a.m. for the students who could afford the luxury of paying others to work for them. This kept me in food and spending money. I ate ramen noodle soup many nights of the week, six packs for a dollar.

With my success at Harvard, I took another risk and applied for a prestigious fel-lowship—much to my surprise, I received a Fulbright Scholarship for independent research in Denmark. Skidmore refused to give me a deferment of my student loan, so nine months of loan repayment had to be covered, eliminating what little I had saved. I went to Denmark with $200 in my pocket and a small monthly stipend for housing and food. Much of the $200 was spent in the first day on items I had been told I would not need, such as blankets and other household items. Their housing plans for me had changed; unfortunately they didn't tell me until I arrived without these items.

Upon my return I worked for ten years at a variety of management jobs in con-tinuing higher education before deciding it was again time to return to school to enable me to move upward professionally. With a full tuition waiver, I pursued and received a Ph.D. in human development at the University of Rochester, and was asked to stay on as a full-time faculty member. The story continues, but this is enough for now. What a strange and unusual journey for a little girl from a blue-collar back-ground living in the swamp.

My doctoral dissertation research focused on the intersection of social class, gender, and education. A subset of that study found, surprisingly, that school personnel—including teachers and counselors—play a role as gatekeepers in our society; specifically, they preserve the status quo by failing to encourage talented youths from lower social classes to "aspire higher," as Jesse Jackson might say. More accurately stated, their interactions with poorer girls in junior high or high school who have demonstrated superior academic achievement is neutral or nega-tive. The following excerpts come from the women I interviewed, women now in professional careers in higher education who range in age from mid-20's to mid-50's. These quotes were in response to the question of who, if anyone, first noticed their potential for achievement.

"When I was going through elementary school ... they basically selected a group of kids in fourth grade ... that they thought were high achievers. They put us together in a special class ... I was in the high track throughout high school. I recognized that, and *every time my counselor tried to put me into another track* [emphasis added], I would go and have an argument with him." (Linda)[1]

"The classes that I was put in [in high school] were the general classes. My guidance counselor in the school didn't recognize any of my awards and things at the eighth-grade level. So I was getting 100's on Latin, 100 in algebra ..." (Sylvia)

"... as far as actually encouraging me personally, no, definitely a lack of that looking back ... No, no one ever said much about college, or really encouraged me, or sat down and said, look at all the choices you have." (Jennifer)

"They never knew quite what to do with me, because I was *not* supposed to do well, because I was from a farm." (Karen) [Karen further noted that the teachers "could identify who they expected to do well and who they didn't" based on their perception of the socioeconomic status of the student's parents.]

"No one was interested. No one was terribly impressed. It was a football high school, you understand." (Marcia)

"I really don't feel as though I got very good guidance in my high school years, because I didn't really know anything about going to college, and I wanted to go. Knowing what I know now, I just made a hundred mistakes and bad choices ... there were people who were very kind to me, but I don't think anyone who you could say mentored me to make sure I took the right courses and did the right things." (Penny) Penny further noted that her peers from higher social classes "came from families who went to college" and thus the counselors "assume you know ... how to apply for colleges, and how to get aid. They just assume everyone else knows it." She continued, "I didn't even know the questions to ask. I didn't know how much I didn't know."

"Even though I was a good student, I was never talked to about college." (Rita)

"I wish I had had better advice when I was in high school, thinking about going to college. I think I would have done better if I'd made a better choice about where to be an undergraduate." (Karen) Karen also noted that her school counselor's knowledge of colleges outside of her geographic area was limited to one, and that knowledge consisted of the fact that "they served beer in the student union."

"The one person that really wasn't all that supportive was the school counselor at the time. [Interviewer: What kind of things did the school counselor say to you?] Well, that I probably would marry a farmer. That if I wanted to go to school, go someplace local. I probably should plan to be a teacher or a nurse … If I talk to women my age … many of them got the same kind of negative reinforcement from counselors." (Polly)

"They were mostly men [the counselors], and they were mostly very negative … I took algebra, trig, advanced algebra, geometry … And they were telling me I ought to go into business, and take shorthand. I knew I should be taking college prep, but I wasn't getting any of that from them …" (Pat)

"… that limited view Mr. _____ had. He was very sexist in his approach to counseling students … [if I had done what he wanted] I would have been a secretary … [If you were female] in high school you had to take the secretarial track." (Pam)

"… a guidance counselor once told me that I'd never go to college, and that I'd never make it in college, I wasn't smart enough. I still, to this day, know his name and I'd love to go back to him and say, you know, "*Now* look!' … You would think a guidance counselor would be motivating kids, not demotivating." (Kim)

I share my story here, and the stories of others, not to portray roles of the victimized but rather to celebrate survivorship. There are no victims in these pages; only survivors who hope to educate others through their narratives of struggle and resilience. I also know that many other talented individuals are not portrayed in these pages because one bad stroke of luck can derail a talented and motivated person from achieving their goals. When your 20-year-old car breaks down and you don't have the $120 for the necessary repair, perhaps you give up your dream to go to college. One health emergency, yours or your child's, when you have no health insurance, can eliminate your college tuition savings account. So, the survivor stories are also for the sake of those who did not make it this far.

I have presented these quotes to you because their direct quality speaks volumes in terms of discrimination in education based on gender and social class. Over the course of three years, I interviewed over twenty women, and the vast majority of them reported this type of discrimination in their early lives, which continued on at the college level.

The voices above speak specifically to less-than-optimal interactions with school counselors. Other respondents reported having no contact at all with their school counselor. This is quite remarkable in and of itself, given that the vast majority of these women were at or near the top of their high school classes. It is tempting to dismiss these reports as time-bound; that is, that these are reports of yesteryear and such things don't happen any longer. However, some of the women were in their 20's at the time of the interview, suggesting a very contemporary experience. Further, more recent reports from young college women in my undergraduate and graduate courses over the past several years suggest that such discouraging interactions continue unabated. The typical limited advice given to such women is to become a teacher, nurse, hairdresser, or secretary; certainly, there is no discussion of college initiated by school personnel.

Gender- and class-based discrimination is not new. A considerable body of research documents the ways in which boys receive more attention in the classroom (and more academically challenging questions and assignments), while girls are dismissed or patronized. Additional literature describes a distressing state of affairs in which children from lower social-class backgrounds receive negative treatment in school based on their attire, speech patterns, and parents' occupational status, regardless of performance on school tasks. Teachers focus on conformity to codes of conduct in children from poor families, while focusing instead on critical thinking skills with children from higher social classes. There is little wonder that given this dual marginality, talented girls from lower social-class backgrounds are either ignored or discouraged from higher achievement. Certainly, boys suffer as well.

Public schools are not alone in their discouragement of the higher aspirations of talented young people from lower social-class backgrounds. Colleges are quite good at letting students know who belongs and who does not. Colleges do not make modifications to suit their prospective or actual clientele; rather, "different" students must change in order to match the cultural norms of the institution. The painful and fundamental process of change which is required of students from lower social-class backgrounds to accommodate to the norms of the middle- to upper-class college environment has been called "resocialization." It may entail relinquishing the tastes and loyalties of the "home" world and becoming "a chameleon," as my interviewees called it, changing in order to fit prevailing standards of dress, speech, and so on. They learn to hide the clues that would let others know of their true roots. The clear message these students receive is that the stigma of lower social-class background is something to be hidden, something of which to be ashamed.

So … what can be done? It became clear in the course of my interviews that social class is simply not talked about in school or college settings in a personalized, meaningful way. It is either avoided completely or discussed in the abstract, "out there"; but for the student, the experience is "in here." Little more than lip service is given to the tremendous structural obstacles faced by individuals from lower social-class backgrounds, which may functionally prevent access to achievement and success. We can all learn more about social class, acknowledge the continuing specter of gender inequality and advocate for change, talk about our own histories and herstories, and make social class an equally addressed dimension of diversity.

When I present on this topic in various venues, at conferences on education or counseling, at colleges and universities or at public schools, I am often met with warmth and relief by the few people there from lower social-class backgrounds. I have been told, "You're telling *my* story!" and "I thought I was all alone ... At last, someone who understands!" However, I am just as frequently met with angry resistance. Individuals from privileged backgrounds do not want to be blamed for the malfunctioning of society, and certainly not for the failures of individuals from disadvantaged backgrounds. This is particularly true as our public schools face poor accountability marks for the unacceptable percentages of children from lower social-class backgrounds who fail to graduate from high school.

One public school administrator said in his evaluation of a workshop I presented on this topic, "I'm sad to know that I will be discriminated against by some because of my privileged background." While I have less sympathy for this statement from a person who has continuously been in a position of privilege, at the same time, the purpose of this book is not to shame a different group of people. Enough shaming has gone on already! Rather, it is to increase awareness of the real issues and the real people who are forced to deal with them. My hope is that raised consciousness will lead to meaningful action towards equality, and several suggestions in this direction are offered in Chapter 8 of this book.

The anger and the resistance with which I am met come from, I think, a variety of places. First of all, my presentations and workshops are often the first encounter that an individual from a higher social-class background has with the concrete realities of discrimination based on social class, and its actual consequences (detailed in later chapters). What they learned in college about social class was abstract and easily ignored as another theoretical construct. The shock of what I refer to as cumulative disadvantage is hurtful to people, painful to accept. There is a recognition on some level that the over-advantaged reality of one person contributes in some way to the very challenged existence of another. I fully believe that most privileged persons do not have the intention of making life miserable for others, for denying others the same advantages that they are happy to have, or of which they are sometimes oblivious. So, my workshops are somewhat of a rude awakening, and there is a clear desire to make me go away, or at least to assert that the information I present must be wrong, that somehow I've got it all wrong. The implication, though, is that if I do have it all wrong, that indeed some people in the room, or children in that school, and their families, are wrong, bad, lazy, stupid losers. This does not fit with the picture they have of themselves or of others. This is what is called "cognitive dissonance" in psychology.

Cognitive dissonance occurs when you are presented with evidence that does not match your currently existing beliefs. An unrelated example from history was the belief that the earth was flat. Evidence was presented that the earth was round, but this new information was met with quite violent opposition for many reasons (some of which were based in religious doctrine of the time). So if you believe that all poor people are probably stupid, lazy, and so on, and I present you with information that in fact, poor people are equally as intelligent and hardworking as everyone else, and that in fact society sets up a series of insurmountable obstacles to this particular group's likelihood of achieving success, then this is pretty hard to swallow. The "dissonance" forces you to consider new ideas that will replace your prior unexamined beliefs. Unless, of course, you're one of those people from a lower social-class background, in which case this information is warmly welcomed and I am elevated to something like sainthood.

I submitted an article on my research to a journal on counseling and counselor education a few years ago. One of the members of the editorial board commented that my findings "must be wrong." In other words, s/he said, what I had written "could not possibly be accurate". This is another great example of cognitive dissonance, combined with power. Editorial board members often come from privileged backgrounds, and prefer not to believe that their privileged positions are unearned, nor that their advantaged location has come at the cost of another person's opportunities.

One of the challenges in working with this information is to figure out how to create a space that is safe for everyone to convene, presumably in the best interests of children, of educational environments, of human services, of global cooperation, of an evolving and ethical society. It sometimes seems like an either/or situation, but you don't have to accept that. If you're reading this book, you are interested in change for the better, so you're already at an advantage because you've noticed that the glass is half full. There's enough for everyone; the trick is in figuring out how to distribute it equally and fairly.

1

USA: Not the classless society

In 1835 and 1840, Frenchman Alexis de Toqueville wrote the two-volume *Democracy in America*, a sociopolitical commentary based on his nine-month visit to the United States in the early 1830's. In his overview and analysis of American culture and what he believed was an historical movement from aristocracy to democracy, he included a chapter entitled, "How Democracy Affects the Relations of Masters and Servants." Toqueville's own experience of his native Europe provided a model in which the master is always and forever master; the servant will always and forever be of an inferior class. Like the caste system in India of the time, there was no possibility of movement upward—you were born into a class and you would die in that class.

What de Toqueville found in America was an ambiguous relationship between equals: the new democratic government was founded on ideals of equality, and in theory any American could be master of his or her own destiny. Yesterday's servant might indeed become tomorrow's master. Today's master might fall to a lower level. Whereas the European model, with its distinct roles and predictable futures, created a likewise predictable type of servant-master relationship, this was not the case in America. Rather, the servant could aspire to the position of master. The master, alas, did not aspire to the role of servant; and thus the stage for subterranean conflict between the classes was set.

This book attempts to describe the reality of social class relationships in America. It is not a history book, nor is it a Marxist analysis of economic relations. It is about real people, their stories, their lives, as they struggle with the reality of class conflict and the myth of upward mobility with which most Americans are raised. Most importantly, it's about how we navigate these realities every day, without thinking about it, without talking about it.

As the "classless society", Americans don't have a vocabulary for talking about social class, nor even a starting place. Part of the purpose for this book is in providing a starting place, and a claim that "the emperor has no clothes." In his 1970 book, *Cultural Action for Freedom*, Paulo Freire refers to a "culture of silence" and the need to subvert that culture in order to overcome ignorance and oppression.[2] A third world exists within our own country, a world in which people are impoverished and denied equal access to education and upward mobility. Now we can admit what many of us have suspected but couldn't say out loud. The United States *is* a deeply class-stratified society. This means that some people get ahead, and others are held back, often unintentionally, but certainly with huge implications in a society presumably based on ideals of equality and justice.

Let's start by looking at the rags-to-riches myths of our culture. This is the basic story line: a young man (it's usually a man) gets a very low-level job in the mail room of a large company. He is clever, honest, and hard-working. Over the years he steadily rises through the ranks until one day, lo and behold, he becomes president of the company, complete with big salary and the office with the best view of the city. Happily ever after, end of story, right?

Not so fast! This story represents one of the most deeply held beliefs of Americans: the myth of the meritocracy. A meritocracy is a system in which individuals get ahead (or not) based on their actual skills and abilities, not because of various connections or unearned privileges based on class. We love this idea because it seems fair and just. The people who get ahead actually deserve to; they earned it. A recent series of articles in the *New York Times* focused on social class, and the myth of upward mobility. "A recent study by the Federal Reserve Bank of Boston found that few families moved from one quintile, or fifth, of the income ladder to another during the 1980's than during the 1970's and that still fewer moved in the 90's than in the 80's. A study by the Bureau of Labor Statistics also found that mobility declined from the 80's to the 90's."[3] The *Times* article also reported on its own poll; and despite statistics to the contrary, a significant percentage of Americans continue to believe that upward mobility is more likely now than ever in our country. The reverse is closer to the truth, and the reality of who achieves upward mobility is considerably more complex.

Unfortunately, many of us have experienced situations where it's not what you know, it's who you know. This is not unusual in the job market. If your father knows the manager of Company X, you might have a better chance of getting a job there, especially if the manager would like to do business with your father in the future. If your father is a service station attendant, it is less likely that he will have the kind of connections necessary to help you to get a professional position. But the job market is not the only place where the myth of the meritocracy plays out.

An excellent example of this is legacy admissions. Legacy admissions are a traditional part of the process for selecting new students to be admitted to prestigious colleges and universities. Typically an elite college will set aside about ten percent of the available spaces for incoming students who are the children of alumni and/or donors to the school. On the surface of it, this doesn't sound too bad. However, when you stop and think about who the alumni are, you see how the same system of privilege is reinforced and recreated through this system. If John Adams went to Ivy University back in the 1800s because of the wealth and privilege of his family (i.e., they could actually afford to pay his tuition, room, and board; and they could also afford to not have him at home doing labor on behalf of the family), then his son automatically had a better chance of being accepted, and the grandson, and the great-grandson, and so on. So, an advantage is given to people who are already advantaged.

In his preface to the 1990 edition of *Reproduction,* Pierre Bourdieu reflected upon the increasing awareness of social reproduction in education, certainly relevant in the case of legacy admissions: "We now know that, in America no less than in Europe, credentials contribute to ensuring the reproduction of social inequality by safeguarding the preservation of the structure of the distribution of powers through a constant re-distribution of people and titles characterized, behind the impeccable appearance of equity and meritocracy, by a systematic bias in favour of the possessors of inherited cultural capital."[4] In other words, people who already have more are in powerful positions to ensure that they get more of the things that are valued in our culture, including educational credentials.

When legacy admission slots are saved for the privileged, you can easily figure out who is going to be excluded. Historically, our finest institutions of higher education were designed for privileged white males. Legacy admissions are particularly harmful to non-whites, and those from disadvantaged backgrounds. If one hundred spaces are available, and ten are set aside for the sons and daughters of privilege, then ten deserving prospective students without that history of advantage will be rejected.

Sometimes the legacy process gives extra points to the children of alumni and donors such that their "merit" is inflated. That is, a "C" student from a legacy family might be admitted when an "A" student from a disadvantaged family is not. Likewise, students who attend expensive private high schools benefit because private schools are often rated more highly than the average public school. The assumption is that a higher quality of education is provided in the elite private school setting than in a public school. Again, more points go to the people who are already winning. So much for the meritocracy in our finest institutions of higher education.

The other important way in which the meritocratic ideal undergirds our social class system has to do with assumptions about people at the lowest socioeconomic levels of our society. If person A starts in the mailroom, and works their way up to the CEO position, we assume that person is hard-working, talented, and motivated. If person B starts in the mailroom and stays there, or worse, gets fired, we assume that person is lazy, stupid, and unmotivated. External factors are ignored. What if person B is discriminated against due to gender, race, or ethnicity? Could that be why she was not promoted? What if person B attended high school in an inner city with poor resources, overcrowded classrooms, and burned-out teachers? What if person B realistically had no chance of attending college due to her family's financial limitations, and thus has very little education?

When we look at individual circumstances, there are often compelling reasons for an individual's under- or unemployment or lack of educational achievement; and these reasons have nothing to do with native intelligence, effort, nor desire to move ahead. However, our tendency is to assume that the people who get ahead in life are those who earned it, who deserve to win. The rags-to-riches myth implies that the losers deserve their lot in life. Or do they?

As sociologist Barbara Peters wrote, "I was told by a psychiatrist that I should not go back to college. He put in my med records that I had delusions of grandeur. I was a single mother, on welfare, and I guess I wasn't supposed to go above my 'station'."[5] The structures of our society are such that the masters continue to win all the prizes, and the servants are excluded from even competing. Servants are branded as servants and are expected to stay in their place. Then, we blame the servants for being so slow and stupid and lazy.

When a person from the working class actually does succeed, that person is typically greeted not with praise and congratulations, but rather with stunned surprise. As Janna[6] related her story,

> Before I became a professional, I worked as a secretary for 25 years. Twelve of those years were spent going to school at night. I was also a single parent. I started out at a community college and then transferred to an Ivy League university where I received my undergraduate and graduate degrees. My employer paid for my tuition. They had no idea that I was preparing to get out of there. I think they expected me to work as a secretary for the rest of my life. They really underestimated my capabilities and motivation, to say the least.... My bosses (doctors and medical directors) were absolutely shocked when I told them I had graduated and was leaving.

When the assumption is that working-class people are unsuccessful due to their own deficits, those who judge their performance find success unexpected and, to some extent, inexplicable in the current framework of the stereotypes they hold. Some people are born on third base and congratulate themselves for reaching home plate; others have to actually hit the ball, run around all the bases, and slide into home covered in dirt and sweat from managing obstacles every step of the way.

When I have presented on this topic to audiences of people from working-class backgrounds, tears are often shed as working-class people tell their stories. Part of the emotion is the release of simple fear and anxiety—this is the first time they felt safe enough to tell their story. Everyone is aware of the shaming that goes on in our culture. What if your father was regularly unemployed? What if your mother was a chambermaid? What if your family never owned a home? What if your clothes all came from the second-hand shop or hand-me-downs? Somehow these truths must be hidden for fear of public humiliation. We are torn between loyalty to those we love (our families) and a society that blames people for their difficult circumstances. *Of course* it's not safe to tell your story, when you know you will be seen as a failure, or your parents viewed as stupid, lazy, unmotivated. Through our belief in the meritocracy—which should perhaps be called the meritocrazy—we reinforce the class-based stigma that says you must be stupid, bad, or just plain wrong-headed if you aren't succeeding. So for someone to tell their story out loud is courageous indeed. You will read many of those stories throughout this book.

Needless to say, of course there are people who are indeed stupid, lazy, and unmotivated. These qualities are not class-bound. We find dolts at all levels of the social class system. Just because someone is wealthy does not mean they are talented, hard-working, or motivated. This is the other side of the coin of social class stereotypes. There seems to be a naïve belief that rich people must be smart, that all students at Yale are geniuses, that all company presidents are brilliant. A fresh example of this appears in the documentary film, *Born Rich.*[7] Young Jamie Johnson, heir to the Johnson & Johnson company fortune, filmed some of his college-age friends who also stand to inherit millions or billions of dollars of family wealth. One young man, Luke, candidly related his experience of "attending" Brown University. As Luke described it, he had actually only attended class a total of eight times. He received some halfhearted warning letters from the Dean encouraging his attendance at class and attention to academics, which he ignored. However, he received passing grades in every course. He was at a loss to explain this himself, other than attributing his academic "success" to his family's astounding wealth.

When you have the advantage of wealth handed down to you, and when you have the privilege of the finest educational credentials money can buy (attendance optional), and when you have exceptional social and professional connections to give you that inside edge for the best jobs available (if you must work), or if you inherit a company, this has little to do with your native abilities or skills. However, this is not discussed in America. We prefer to cling to our belief in the meritocracy. After all, it's only fair. Or is it?

This book is based on my research with women from blue-collar backgrounds who became higher education professionals (faculty members or administrators). I initially conducted a pilot study with five women who assisted me in identifying initial directions for inquiry. I then convened a focus group of six women who began the next phase of my research through discussion and shaped the form of further individual interviews which I conducted with ten women. The focus of my study was on the lived experience of these women. It was about the richness of their lives, and the meaning of the incidents of their lives as they understood those situations. The pain that they endured as they attempted to realize the American dream is chronicled in these pages.

At the outset, interviewees were assured that every attempt would be made to protect their privacy and provide anonymity. Accordingly, pseudonyms are employed throughout this book. Geographic location and other identifying features of the institutions attended by the participants and at which they are or have previously been employed are likewise disguised. Although the specific positions held by the participants would be helpful points of interest to the reader, as they were to the author, they must also be obscured to protect the identities of the women. Specifically, women in some administrative roles or specialty areas in academe are uncommon enough across the United States that even indirect reference to them might be sufficient to identify an individual. The privacy of these women is of greater importance than whatever small benefit might accrue from the reader's knowledge of their exact position title or institutional location.

Although the book is based on research about women's experiences, this is not to say that it is irrelevant to men. Much, if not all, of the experiences described pertain to men from lower social-class backgrounds also. The women I interviewed represented a variety of racial and ethnic groups; however, the majority were white. I made a conscious effort to see each person as a unified whole, rather than fragmenting the narratives—and thus, the person—based on perspectives of race and ethnicity. I believe that the value of the unified whole, and the themes related to social class and education in particular, have relevance for all people from lower social-class backgrounds; but I would go further to say that the material presented herein has relevance to all people who want to live in an equal and just society, regardless of the important and unique characteristics of race, ethnicity, and gender.

While this book will have appeal for many audiences, the book is written especially for professional educators, human services personnel, and mental health professionals (counselors in particular). I believe that an ounce of prevention is worth a pound of cure; thus, the changes that must be made in our society to realize our shared vision of justice and equality must begin at a very fundamental level and at the earliest stages of life. Therefore, professionals whose work is with children and families are critical to this effort. College personnel and human resource professionals will also find this of value as you work with college students and entry-level employees.

The first section of the book discusses the concept of social class and why we should concern ourselves with this issue. In the second section of the book, I address the specific ways in which class makes a difference, from birth through college and career choices, particularly in educational environments. The third section focuses on the stories of the women I interviewed, as well as other men and women who have shared their stories with me in the past few years. The patterns and themes that emerge are profiled in this section. The final section of the book includes suggestions for proactive policies and practices.

2

Social Class: A Moveable Feast?

So, what *is* "social class," anyway? This is an important and complex question. If you ask five sociologists to define social class, you'll get five different definitions. This chapter attempts to clarify what we're talking about when we discuss social class issues.

First, let's consider historical and global contexts. The concept of class has been around since the time of the Romans. According to the *International Encyclopedia of Sociology*, "Roman census-takers introduced the term *classis* when differentiating the population on the basis of wealth for purposes of military service obligation. Its use in English for classes in society (as distinct from classes in schools or as a part of a classification of plants etc.) is associated with the beginning of the Industrial Revolution in the 18th century."[8]

In India, the *caste* system is a clearly delineated type of social organization, much like classes but without the possibility of movement from one segment to another. Some would argue that the rigidity of the American class system is very similar to that in India[9]; we just don't like to admit it. Many cultures have varying degrees of social stratification, and there is varying acceptance of those divisions in society. Much of the Western conception of social class has been based on the works of Karl Marx and Max Weber, both of whom focused on economics. However, Marx and Weber had distinctly different views on class, and so contemporary thought is likewise divergent.

Despite these differences, it is important to have a shared definition, a starting point, for any discussion of social class issues. One definition of "class" that encompasses both Marxian and Weberian thought is this: "A form of social stratification in which allocation to, membership of, and relationships between classes are governed by economic considerations rather than law (as in estates) or religion and ritual pollution (as in caste)."[10]

A less formal, but equally valid definition of class would be this:

Money + Power + Prestige = Class Position/Rank.

A recent series of articles on social class in the *New York Times* also attempts to explain what "class" is: "Class is rank, it is tribe, it is culture and taste. It is attitudes and assumptions, a source of identity, a system of exclusion. To some, it is just money."[11] *Times* article authors Scott and Leonhardt go on to say, "Classes are groups of people of similar economic and social position—people who, for that reason, may share political attitudes, lifestyles, consumption patterns, cultural interests and opportunities to get ahead."[12] This latter point is important, because class position greatly influences prospects for upward mobility.

Several possible definitions of "class" have been presented. There are some basic elements to help understand what class really means. Social classes are hierarchically arranged economic groupings in an overall system. The economic sorting criteria that are used typically include: level of education, level of income, type of occupation, housing/property, and the associated prestige or status that accompanies each of these factors. Contemporary writers, such as Pierre Bourdieu, also include "cultural capital"; that is, as alluded to in the *Times*, the tastes of individuals and goods acquired according to what is valued in the society. Much of the criteria for determining class standing are also related to power dynamics in the social group or society. In other words, individuals with power tend to dictate what is valued in the society.

Over time, with changes in patterns of labor (from farming, to industrial, to information technology) also have come finer distinctions in occupational status. In the past, white-collar laborers typically had greater prestige than blue-collar workers, who were clearly performing manual labor; however, in today's workplace many white-collar jobs are minimum-wage dead-end occupations with no upward mobility or economic improvement (for example, the so-called pink-collar ghetto of the bank teller or data-entry clerk). Even managers may have little economic or status advantage in chain stores or like industries.

The term "underclass" is a newer concept. This is sometimes used to describe the long-term poor who are denied full participation or citizenship in society. It includes the unemployed, underemployed, working poor. It often overlaps with other social categories of race and gender. The status of this group and their economic deprivation causes their exclusion from the benefits and gains of an overall affluent society.[13]

Some sociologists suggest there are several social class groupings, even as many as nine. The *New York Times* referred to the "big three" commonly accepted class distinctions as upper, middle and working classes.[14] Beeghley suggested that there are four major classes in American society[15]:

Rich	5% of the population
Middle Class	50%
Working class	35%
Poor	10%

While this structure is a helpful starting point for understanding class hierarchy, there are problems with this outline. There is not wide agreement on what "working class" or "middle class" means, nor even "rich" and "poor". There may be geographic variations, as well as urban/rural distinctions. In short, it is a moveable feast: it changes with what one brings to the table in terms of perspective, information, and—most importantly—interpretation.

A brief example may help to illustrate this point. In the rural blue-collar town where I grew up, a hairdresser was a woman (certainly not a man) who stood on her feet for about ten hours a day, essentially making little more than minimum wage and with no prestige in the community based on her occupation. In Hollywood or Beverly Hills or in Manhattan, a hair stylist (title correction) is a man or woman who often works in an elegant setting with a clientele of individuals who are willing to pay significant amounts of money for his/her attention. The stylist has minions to help with the lower-level tasks of shampooing and sweeping up. This stylist may be included in the social connections of their upper-class clients, and thus garner significant cultural capital as well. So you can see that there are differences in status and income even within one occupational title. It would be difficult to accurately place a "hair stylist" on the social class scale without taking into account the context in which that person operates.

Not all views of the meaning and measurement of social class are equally valid. If you're reading books on social class issues, look for data and/or sources provided by the author to back up any claim of a definition of social class. Consider the possible bias of the writer in evaluating these definitions. Many highly trained social scientists come from privileged backgrounds themselves and may not have the objective perspective that they claim. It is in the best interests of certain segments of the population to keep social class an abstract topic that cannot be discussed concretely because it cannot be accurately defined. If it cannot be approached, there is little chance of action on behalf of those whose lives are negatively impacted by class inequities and class bias.

Another complicating factor is that many individuals and families identify themselves as middle class, although objective measures would place them in another category. Both poor and rich will often say that they're middle class. This seems puzzling at first glance, but there may be good reason for this error in self-reporting. Obviously, for the poor there is some stigma associated with being poor, for the reasons discussed previously with regard to the mistaken attributions that come with poverty. There is also some likelihood that there is some discomfort or shame as well that comes with extreme wealth. In our current economic system, while there is enough for all, the wealth of one requires the poverty of another.

Yet another semantic issue comes with the term, "working class". Many middle class individuals call themselves working class, and depending on individual situations this may be consistent with Marxist theory. If they are not the owners of their own businesses, and thus destinies, they are workers and so define themselves as working class. However, the CEO of a major corporation could call himself working class by virtue of the fact that he is an employee of a company, regardless of the fact that he is paid millions of dollars per year in salary. This makes self-definition problematic, and it is clearly necessary to always take context into account when considering class location.

In talking about social class issues, it is often helpful to identify what *you* believe it means, and to negotiate a shared definition in order to facilitate discussion. This brings clarity and helps to avoid needlessly offending other discussants. There are many resources in the literature if you would like to explore this complex concept further.

In my own work, due to the complexity of the term, "social class," I decided to use "blue-collar" as a descriptor when I sought women to interview. This seemed less ambiguous. I specifically looked for women who came from blue-collar backgrounds; that is, that one or both of their parents were employed in manual-labor occupations. I also specified that, in order to be included in the study, their parents had not completed college. Additional narratives have been contributed by men and women who define themselves as working-class academics, and whose backgrounds clearly fall within the same category as my original interviewees. In this book, I use the terms blue-collar, lower social class, and working-class interchangeably. It is important to note that when I use the term "lower class", this is not pejorative in any sense; rather, this is a reflection of the class hierarchies and economic realities just discussed. I am not implying that some persons are "lesser than" others based on their class location nor that others are "better" because they are "upper class".

Finally, in my research I interviewed women who were currently employed in higher education as faculty members or administrators. Based on research on occupational prestige (covered in more depth in Chapter 3), we know that professions in higher education are highly valued in our culture, and thus have great status. The high contrast between the world of the interviewees' origins and their current employment location was of interest to me, and I felt this would emphasize the meaning of social class disparities in our culture and in their lives. This is explored in greater depth in the coming chapters.

PART II

Human development in the context of class-stratified culture

3

The "leaky pipeline": How class operates in cultural and institutional settings

This chapter will focus on education as an example of a socially valued location in which class issues shape both individual and group outcomes. Schools and colleges are a reflection of the values of the larger culture. We will examine documented disparities in educational attainment based on social class, as well as barriers to both access and achievement in education. For example, less than one in four individuals successfully complete a baccalaureate degree; those who do are disproportionately white and middle- or upper-class[16]. These disparities are huge and growing.

Like career pathways, educational attainment has been called a "leaky pipeline"[17]. Specifically, the puzzling fact is that women entering graduate study in the sciences drop out at a much higher rate than males; in addition, while women populate the halls of many corporations, relatively few garner management positions. In careers and in graduate study in chemistry, engineering, medicine, and like endeavors, if 100 students begin a program—50 females and 50 males—only about 25 females will finish the program, whereas about 35 males will complete the program. The women are "leaking out" of the pipeline of education for some reason, and since presumably they were bright and capable enough to complete undergraduate degrees, their failure to complete the advanced degree might have something to do with the institution, our culture, or other issues.

Similarly, the leaky pipeline exists from elementary school onward. Otherwise bright and capable youngsters become disenfranchised, disengaged, disinterested. While we can all agree that some students are simply lacking in talent (and this occurs across social class categories), this could not account for the epidemic of dropouts and low performers in school. What might be the other reasons for this?

Why is education important as a way to understand social class issues in America? Not only is it a place where we spend much of our time for about 13 years of our life, but as a society, we seem to have decided that education is central to our values.

The National Opinion Research Center (NORC) has been conducting polls for quite some time now on what are the "best jobs in America"[18]. This research is repeated at regular intervals. Basically NORC researchers provide each survey participant with a stack of index cards. On each card is a job title. The survey participant is asked to rank order the cards according to their own sense of what the "best jobs" are. Table 3.1 below includes a sample of some job titles. Take a moment to think about how you might rank order these.

Table 3.1 Sample list of unranked jobs from NORC study[19]

Accountant
Airplane Mechanic
Assembly Line Worker
Baker
Banker
Bank Teller
Barber
Bartender
Bill Collector
Bus Driver
Cashier in a Supermarket
Chemist
Clergyman
Cook in a Restaurant
Department Head in a State Government
Farm Owner and Operator
Filling Station Attendant
Gardener
General Manager of a Manufacturing Plant
House Painter
Housekeeper in a Private Home
Insurance Agent
Janitor
Lawyer
Locomotive Engineer

Logger
Lunchroom Operator
Manager of a Supermarket
Medical Technician
Musician in a Symphony Orchestra
Policeman
Public Grade School Teacher

Once you have made a rank ordering, look at the top three jobs you selected. Why did you choose these? Is there any underlying theme or pattern as to why you thought these were the "best jobs" in America? Now look at the bottom three jobs in your ranking. Why do you think these are the least desirable jobs? What are the common elements?

When I do this exercise with a variety of audiences, including both undergraduate and graduate students, and professionals in education, the results are often the same: the top choices are in the lawyer-doctor-government leader range, and the bottom choices are the service occupations such as filling station attendant, waitress, and janitor.

Table 3.2 shows how this sample actually was ranked by the thousands of Americans who have participated in this survey over the past few decades. How do these results compare to your list?

Table 3.2 Sample list of jobs ranked in NORC study[20]

Department Head in a State Government
Lawyer
Chemist
Medical Technician
Clergyman
Accountant
Public Grade School Teacher
Banker
General Manager of a Manufacturing Plant
Policeman
Musician in a Symphony Orchestra
Airplane Mechanic
Farm Owner and Operator
Manager of a Supermarket
Locomotive Engineer

Insurance Agent
Bank Teller
Barber
Baker
Assembly Line Worker
Cook in a Restaurant
Housekeeper in a Private Home
House Painter
Cashier in a Supermarket
Bus Driver
Logger
Gardener
Lunchroom Operator
Bartender
Bill Collector
Janitor
Filling Station Attendant

Some thinking about why Americans rank these jobs in the way they do is in order. Certainly, those same elements of social class that were discussed previously make their appearance here: income for the job, prestige of the job, level of education required for the job. There is also something more, and this is an essential concept: control over information. What do I mean by this?

Let's say you had been feeling ill, and you went to see your doctor. You are going to your doctor, rather than the filling station attendant, because your doctor has been highly educated regarding diseases and treatments. Your doctor also has the option to share the information s/he has with you, or not. This may sound like an odd thing to even think about. Consider this: Historically, when women had cancer, the physician would often tell the husband the diagnosis, and the prognosis, and they would not tell the patient because they did not want to worry her! In other words, the woman was treated like a child who had no authority over her own health status, nor the ability to make appropriate choices given the facts about her health situation.

In another scenario, imagine you have been accused of committing a crime. You are, in fact, innocent. You hire a lawyer, or one is assigned to you. Presumably this individual has studied the law, and knows the legal statutes relevant to your case, and how to proceed in a court of law. Again, you are relying upon this individual's knowledge and their likelihood of sharing with you, and the court, information that is appropriate and relevant to your case. It is not only their knowledge base that is important, but their power over how to disseminate this information is very important to your future—a future that might be spent behind bars, or as a free person. So you see how this essential concept applies; that control over information is really about power, and in these cases, this power may be literally over life or death, freedom or imprisonment. So, what does this have to do with education?

The categories of jobs that are not reflected in the NORC sample tables and which are, in fact, the highest ranked jobs in America, are *teachers of* those other "best" jobs. That is, a teacher of lawyers, a teacher of doctors, a teacher of government leaders; these are the "best jobs" in America. The amount of information these teachers control is mind-boggling. So, the "best jobs in America" are those of teachers at the highest levels of education. It is no wonder, then, that educational institutions are at the center of our culture and reflect our most highly prized values, and also perhaps, our deepest fears about power and control over life and death and freedom.

In 1991, Judith Touchton and Lynne Davis completed a study of the educational achievement of women in America. They found that 24% of white men and 16% of white women had successfully completed 4 years or more of college (at least a baccalaureate degree)[21]. Thus, fewer than one in five white women had completed a four-year degree. For non-whites, of course, these numbers are much lower due to unequal access and other issues related to discrimination.

More recent information compiled by the Postsecondary Education Opportunity Group indicates that educational attainment has, indeed, increased over the past fifteen years. Of persons in the United States who are age 25 or older, 21.1% had achieved a bachelor's degree or higher in 1989; by 2004 that had increased to 27.7%.[22] Still, that means that only slightly more than one in every four Americans is earning a bachelor's degree, and that says nothing about social class distinctions. It further says nothing about geographic distinctions. Interestingly, the District of Columbia has consistently held the number one spot in the country for highest rates of baccalaureate degree acquisition with 35.2% in 1989 and 45.7% in 2004—impressive indeed. On the other end of the spectrum, West Virginia has fairly consistently held the number 51 spot in the nation with 11.1% of the population earning a bachelor's degree in 1989, increasing to 15.3% in 2004.[23] The key point here is that across our country, more than 70% of Americans age 25 and over have *not* earned a bachelor's degree.

Three additional types of information further supplement our understanding of why such discrepancies exist in educational attainment, and these have to do with access. They are: tuition rates, financial aid, and government financial support for higher education.

It has been said that there are only two sure things in life: death and taxes. I would add a third certainty to that list: tuition increases. The Washington Higher Education Coordinating Board has been compiling tuition rate comparisons by state for some years. In the most recent four-year period for which data is available, 2000-2004, the national percentage increase in resident undergraduate tuition and fees at flagship universities was a staggering 43%.[24] This didn't happen all at once, of course; incremental increases have been occurring yearly and add up to this unfortunate rate. This also varies widely by state, as did the rates of baccalaureate degree attainment. In fact, Hawaii's state university tuition increased only 13.4% in that time period; while Kansas' increased by a whopping 73.8%.[25]

Obviously, with these rather significant tuition increases in our 50 states, one would hope for equivalent increases in state support for higher education. Unfortunately, this is not the case. I used to say that I went to college in the "heyday" of financial aid. As a person from a poor family, low state college tuition and adequate financial aid were absolutely essential to my attendance at college. What I experienced on a personal level is borne out in the data collected by the Center for Higher Education and Education Finance at Illinois State University, and compiled by Nicole Brunt of the Postsecondary Education Opportunity research group. In examining state and local tax fund appropriations for higher education per $1000 of state personal income in fiscal years 1961 through 2005, we find that the low point of $3.69 (per $1000 of state personal income) came in 1961. The rate consistently increased over the next 15 years, reaching a high of $10.58 in 1976, the year I graduated from college. Sadly, the rate then consistently decreased to a low of $6.86 in 2004. It is a simple comparison to examine the figures of tuition increase in the United States and the now declining state support for higher education to see what a difficult situation we have created in terms of the affordability of education for students from economically disadvantaged backgrounds.

The ability to pay is closely linked with access to the best colleges and universities. This could be mediated by the availability of adequate financial aid, so that not only the wealthy could go to college at our finest institutions. There are two kinds of financial aid: merit-based and need-based. As the name would imply, merit-based aid presumably goes to individuals who have distinguished themselves academically or in the arts or sports arena. Need-based aid is awarded to individuals whose assessed economic situation dictates the critical need for financial support to attend college. Financial aid can come from private sources, such as highly specialized scholarships; or from state or federal sources. Aid can also be awarded by the college itself. In *The Student Aid Game,* McPherson and Schapiro analyze both merit- and need-based aid in higher education and conclude that "the larger forces at work right now in American higher education … will tend to increase the gaps between the 'haves' and the 'have-nots' among institutions and between the more and the less needy among college students. These forces include a withering of public financial support for higher education …"[26] Colleges and universities are in a battle for survival as well, and they are active in devising strategies for getting as much aid as possible from state and federal governments, as well as private donors. However, they are much at the mercy of the politics of higher education finance, and their losses are passed on to students—or in this case, to prospective students who may not attend college due to inadequate aid in the face of stunning tuition and fees. So the term "withering" utilized by McPherson and Schapiro is quite appropriate to our examination of the college attendance rates of students from lower social-class backgrounds.

Thomas Mortensen examined the baccalaureate degree completion rates of students based on family income from 1970 through 2003. Students who came from families in the highest income brackets were far more likely to complete a bachelor's degree by age 24 than were students from any other group. Specifically, Mortensen divided family income into quartiles and compared this with college completion rates, based on Census Bureau data. The probability of attaining a bachelor's degree if you were in the bottom family income quartile was 8.6%. In the second family income quartile, which we might identify as the working class, your chances rose to 13.2%. In the third quartile, presumably the middle class category, you had a 27.7% chance of completing a bachelor's degree; and in the top family income quartile, you had a 74.9% chance of baccalaureate completion.[27] Clearly this data illustrates the reality of unequal educational attainment as linked with wealth and access to educational opportunity, and the information presented does not address the important inequities in access and attainment based on gender, race, and ethnicity.

When I share this information with various groups, they are often quite surprised and disbelieving. Many of the groups to which I speak are college-educated, and so it seems to them that college attendance is the norm, although of course it is not. Everyone knows lots of people who went to college. We tend to socialize and work with others like us, but there is another world out there of people for whom college attendance was not the norm.

In any case, going to college and completing college are not the same thing! Persistence in college is an important factor as well, and may be influenced by finances, intra- and inter-personal issues, and larger cultural forces. As we will see in the following chapter, the culture of the college environment is often unfamiliar and extremely uncomfortable for individuals from lower social-class backgrounds.

When students go off to college, there is an expectation that they will conform to the culture of the host institution. This requires "resocialization" of students who come from backgrounds and homes with different values and practices. Resocialization is a term which was developed from the ideas of German economist and social historian, Max Weber; and essentially means that you must conform to the values and norms of your new environment, or fail. Failure in this context may mean choosing to leave the new environment and return to a familiar one, which affirms and validates your values and behaviors.

The design of higher education institutions has assumed that the populations they serve are homogeneous[28], making them less likely to recognize diversity and act to serve diverse populations appropriately. This homogeneity reflects certain class values. The culture of higher education is primarily reflective of middle- or upper-class values. College practices, philosophies, and environments were historically shaped by and oriented towards privileged European (i.e., white) males; thus their functioning, changed little over the past century, underscores class privilege and male dominance and is therefore particularly oppressive to women. Beyond gender, of course, these values are clearly oppressive of non-whites and of the lower class.

O'Barr makes the point that higher education institutions hold the power to grant degrees, and therefore implicitly demand conformity and silence—not questioning—from students who do not fit the assumed model[29]. The institution is not going to be modified; any alterations to be made will be made by (or to) the student.

London discusses the resocialization of blue-collar students in his work focusing particularly on first-generation college students; that is, students whose parents did not attend college. If, as Weber said, the chief social function of education is to provide socialization into the culture of a social class[30], then this is indeed a jarring experience for first-generation lower-class students. "To be accepted as a full member of a status group and to share with others a sense of membership in it, regardless of its prestige or power, requires socialization into its culture: its styles of language, dress, aesthetic tastes, values, manners, conversational topics, and preferences in sports, media and the arts"[31]. If your preference in sports is bowling and you are surrounded by students whose taste is for playing squash or rowing on the crew team, you might feel out of place. When students talk about Picasso and Renoir and you have little or no training in art history or art appreciation, you might feel like quite a buffoon. Certainly, you might feel quite inferior to your peers, and a profound sense of not fitting in.

Faced with a cultural ethic of individualism where individual achievement is attributed to intelligence, diligence, and self-control, blue-collar students are doomed to blame failure on themselves and their own shortcomings, rather than any shortcomings of the educational institution. Many college students are between the ages of 18 and 21, and don't have the life experience nor maturity nor self-esteem to take a perspective that "I'm OK no matter what these other people think." Rather, they may decide to just go home.

To succeed, students must accept the socialization practices of the larger culture; in this case, the culture of the higher education institution. Students are placed in an ambiguous position between home/family/friends and success in college. To accommodate the practices and tastes of the college culture means modifying or abandoning the practices and tastes of the home culture. "The cultural challenges faced by first-generation students are not limited to the classroom but include the difficulties of redefining relationships and self-identity"[32]. This daily adaptation involves some degree of changing individual identity in order to fit in, and may be quite painful.

One may reasonably ask why students would suffer the indignities of renegotiating identity and relationships with self and others. In 1994, the Gallup Organization published results of a national survey of Americans' levels of confidence in a variety of social institutions. Higher education institutions enjoyed a very high level of the public's confidence, particularly private higher education[33]. This provides some indication of the credibility held by higher education in our society, such that individuals are willing to go to great lengths of personal sacrifice and change in order to conform to its standards.

It is not unusual for students from blue-collar backgrounds to find the college experience to be intimidating and rejecting of their most prized values. They are forced to make a difficult choice between maintaining loyalty to their home community and, in some sense, their own identity; or in betraying those loyalties and adopting a new set of values that is consistent with the college culture.

Students' reactions to the overwhelmingly class-based philosophies, values and practices of educational institutions from the elementary years on include: lower self confidence, feelings of inadequacy and inferiority, lower motivation, lower participation rates, lower achievement, distrust of the system, anger, disillusionment, and alienation. While they would not use these terms to describe it, the place of servant and master is reinforced—and enforced—in educational environments. In the next chapter, we will take a look at how this occurs, step by painful step.

4

Nuts and bolts: Human development in context of family and school

So far we've looked at what social class is, and why educational institutions are a good place to look at how class-based discrimination takes place. In this chapter you'll see how these components work together to create an accumulation of disadvantage for young people from lower social-class backgrounds.

This chapter uses a chronological approach from birth through college to examine each stage of schooling and parallel stages of human development as they are influenced and constrained by social class realities. Examples from interviewees and others will be used to illustrate each stage.

Infancy through Preschool

Where does social class come from? Every child is born into, or placed through adoption with, a family. The child "inherits" the social class standing of the family; specifically, of his/her parents. Many cities and towns are geographically segregated into neighborhoods that bear the social class markers of its inhabitants. These local distinctions may determine access to certain kinds of stores for food and clothing, or even options for childcare or family entertainment. This varies widely depending on the city/town. Almost certainly, access to quality public schools is influenced heavily by these distinctions.

Surprisingly, even preschoolers develop a consciousness of social class distinctions fairly early in life. While adults are more focused on verbal communication, small children may be more aware of certain non-verbal cues from passersby on the streets, stares at mother's clothing or father's rusty car, or even where the family sits in church. They experience a sense of exclusion and difference based on how their family is treated by society, although they would not be able to articulate this as a social class issue.

Much research indicates that gender-role expectations are more strictly adhered to in working-class families; although this is not universally agreed upon. These expectations can influence later achievement behaviors, but are also visible at earlier ages and stages of development. Little girls may be encouraged to do or imitate "homemaker" kinds of things, such as playing with dolls or baking. Little boys may be encouraged towards more active, individual pursuits, such as building forts and houses (even with toy blocks and the like) and being allowed more independent time outdoors. These early influences shape behaviors when the child goes to school.

In the typical blue-collar home, learning stimuli are lacking. For example, there are fewer books in the home, less light, and dull or grayish colors. These are reflective of the limited material conditions of families with low incomes. One interviewee, Eileen, recalled bitterly, "I grew up with a furnace in the living room. The wallpaper was Owens-Corning fiberglass insulation. That was my wallpaper[34]".

Dee wrote, "One of the things I hated most about my childhood was the way my father let our house and belongings deteriorate (this was the only thing about him I disliked; he was otherwise my hero). We didn't quite have junk cars parked on cinder blocks in the yard, but there were piles of stuff in the garage and back yard. Things were just left to rust where they were last dropped (unmown grass usually hid them, though). Even as a child, I swore that if I ever got out of there and had my own house that I would keep it spotless[35]".

The level of material deprivation ranges widely in lower social-class homes. Not many would argue that this lack of basic necessities has an effect on the physically and psychologically developing child. The journal, *American Psychologist* published an article in March 2004 which said, in part,

> Low-income children are read to relatively infrequently, watch more TV, and have less access to books and computers. Low-income parents are less involved in their children's school activities. The air and water poor children consume are more polluted. Their homes are more crowded, noisier, and of lower quality. Low-income neighborhoods are more dangerous, offer poorer municipal services, and suffer greater physical deterioration. Predominantly low-income schools and day care are inferior.[36]

So even in early childhood the poverty of place affects the wellness of children and indirectly, their ability to later succeed in school. Physical factors in the environment are important to the child's physical development. The chaos of a parent's unemployment, underemployment, or multiple changes in employment and working hours may be quite stressful for a young child, making for a worldview in which instability is the norm.

There are numerous interesting patterns about communication and language in the lower-class family that have long-lasting impacts on the developing child. In such homes, there is less verbal interaction both at home and at daycare or preschool[37]. In addition, children may be punished for initiating dialog, as this may appear as insolence to the parent[38]. So if the child asks, as children do, "Daddy, why is the sky blue?", the father may feel this is the child's way of trying to show how ignorant the father is, who, like most of us after all, does not know the answer to this perennial question. So, the child may be yelled at or punished in other ways, and over time the child learns not to ask interesting questions. This self-monitoring and silencing is problematic for later school achievement, where such questions are important and indicative of intelligence, as well as simply necessary for learning what one does not know.

Similarly, the question-and-answer format that is typical of school classrooms is not typical of blue-collar homes. Middle- and upper-class homes typically include this kind of dialog as a sort of scaffolding, a way to teach children to think about the world around them and to investigate, through conversation, how things work.

The silencing that results from punishment for insolence may result in language delays. Children must use words and combine them in interesting ways to learn their effects. If they are not allowed to speak, or if they learn to silence themselves, they will arrive at school behind their classmates in language development and communication ability. This leads to lower achievement, as well as possible problems in social development.

Working-class children are often perceived by teachers as having lower cognitive abilities because of language delays, and thus the child is judged negatively. There are not necessarily cognitive deficits—i.e, in intelligence or capacity for reasoning—but language delays give the appearance of the child processing information slowly because they are not used to responding verbally or to the question-and-answer format.

Based on the geographic or neighborhood distinctions mentioned previously, there may be local dialects used in poorer communities that are likewise judged negatively by teachers. The debate in recent years over the use of Ebonics or "Black English" has highlighted the ways in which public schools privilege a certain standard for the English language, and variations valued in local communities may be rejected in the classroom. Thus, the language that is primary for a child, the language which is spoken in his/her home, may not be the language which is valued and used in school.

A final interesting factor in considering the relevance of social class to early childhood development has to do with the practice of "holding back" a child from entering kindergarten until s/he is "ready." The notion of "not ready" is, in fact, a function of the resources of a family for keeping a child at home and either paying a caregiver or having a family member stay out of the workforce to care for a young child. For many families, it is not possible to stay home another year for a child to be "ready," whatever that might mean. Parents need to work, childcare may not be available or is too costly to be practical. I know in my own circumstance, I went to kindergarten at age four because my mother was, indeed, "ready" for me to go!

Early schooling: Kindergarten through elementary years

Geographic distinctions at this level of development and entry into formal schooling take on a greater importance. Small towns or urban neighborhoods are often homogeneous and working-class or poor areas have limited resources. Public schools in such locations have more difficulty in attracting high-quality teaching staff and administrators, who may prefer the suburbs or whatever other location offers higher quality surroundings and the likelihood of safe parking. School facilities may be maintained at lower levels due to restricted budgets, as public schools function on budgets based at least in part on local property taxes. In better neighborhoods, you see newer and larger facilities. You might see a large football stadium, paid for through donations of parents who can afford to make such large donations. In poor towns and neighborhoods, you see schools with more cracked windows, leaking roofs, and a lack of physical education facilities. Inside there are fewer books, computers, and other resources for learning. Classrooms are more crowded, hallways more chaotic.

Teachers' perceptions of students' abilities are biased by their knowledge of families' socioeconomic status and possibly even their parents' academic histories. Buying into the culture's myths of the relationship between success and ability, students may be assumed to be on the same road as their parents, to failure. Students even at young ages are aware of unfairness and bias in treatment, but are powerless to do anything about it.

In decades past, tracking was openly discussed and thought of as a progressive strategy for providing appropriate instruction to classrooms segregated by ability. Today, tracking has fallen into disfavor, but it certainly still occurs. Tracking begins in the lower grades and is based on perceived ability differences[39]. So based on what was previously discussed about language differences, silencing, and lack of familiarity with the question-and-answer format, you might be able to guess which children are sorted into the "slow" reading group very early on in the elementary grades. Once a child is branded with membership in the slow group, it's very unlikely that s/he will be promoted to a significantly higher level in succeeding years.

Maura shared with me a story of how tracking occurred in her experience assisting in a classroom:

> I saw this when I worked in Title I programs—the students assigned to me for special help were not middle class students, and they were being separated out into a program that ensured that they would stay behind their classmates. Frequently teachers told me they just felt uncomfortable with the students, that they didn't know what to do with them. For example, one teacher felt creepy around a student who had handed back an optional book order form because he said his family couldn't afford it. He didn't even take the form home, he just gave it back to her and she was horrified! How could parents share their financial situation with a 7 year old, she wondered. And surely they could afford a *book*! He was a bright kid and the only reason *at all* that I could see why he had been assigned to Title I was that as the teacher told me, 'I just feel uncomfortable around him.' I don't blame the teacher—she had no more control over her reaction than I did when I entered the classroom and before I knew who I would be working with, spotted this kid—was drawn to him and hoped I would work with him.... Unfortunately, neither I or that teacher had been taught to recognize our reactions for what they were or to understand them and learn to deal with them to the benefit of all students. That's something we have to do on our own.[40]

It is becoming more widely known that non-white children are disproportionately labeled as "special education" students; this appears to be an example of the insidious nature of class bias in marking children as defective due solely to their class background.

Working-class children show limited use of language to express emotions[41]. However, this is a difference in style, not ability. Similar to the discussion of Ebonics noted previously, there is the concept of a "speech community"—a valued style of both verbal and non-verbal expression including a certain dialect and particular meanings for words and phrases that are shared by the community. If the speech community is not recognized by school personnel, it may be disrespected and devalued. This sets up a conflict for the child in which they have to choose their language. They can betray their home language and adopt "school talk," or remain loyal to their speech community and be less successful in school. Some children become bi-dialectal; that is, they have a language for home and another language for school. Not all children are able to—or want to—develop this ability. A third option is taken by some: silence.

Working-class children are easily able to answer concrete questions, such as who, what, when, and where; but they often have difficulty with more abstract thinking, the "why" of things. This is because at home, dialog is concrete and is often one-way: "Do this," "Don't do that." Karen said, "My dad truly never spoke much. Language was used to communicate quite specific things, but not to communicate any sort of inner life or any intellectual life at all; so, you didn't have a language to do that ... And so, that language is different. I mean, it's just not the same[42]".

To school personnel, working-class children sometimes don't seem to make sense. They appear illogical. This may be because middle- and upper-class individuals learn to describe events in a linear sequence: first you do step one, then you do step two, and so on. Working-class children's narratives may appear random because they are not in linear sequence[43]. This matches their home style of narrative. So, if a young child is telling about taking a bath, s/he might start with toweling off, and then return to the use of soap, followed by running the water, interspersed with some details about koolaid which may seem to the listener to be irrelevant. To succeed in school, children have to learn both abstract thinking and also linear sequencing of narrative information. This is quite a challenge for young children, particularly if this linearity is not reinforced at home. The alternative, however, is to be perceived as stupid—failing at logical reasoning and at appropriate narrative structures which are required in school.

Even at the elementary school level, children learn that to be successful in school, they have to learn school-approved modes of interaction, even if that means betraying your family, community, and your own identity. Charlene said, "I feel like I've become an elitist, because when I go home and I listen to my family talk, and they talk in that working class sort of dialect ... it makes me so crazy that they talk in that manner. And then I get mad at them for sounding so stupid. [laughs—then with seriousness] And [I say to myself], don't do that; don't do that you your own family[44]".

Teachers expect inferior performance from working-class children. This becomes a self-fulfilling prophecy, as children are not immune to the negative perceptions and biases of the authority figures around them. "A cardinal principle of sociological social psychology is that an individual tends to become the kind of person [s]he is expected to be as an occupant of a social position with a consistently and clearly defined social role[45]". However, sometimes there are surprises. When working-class students meet higher standards, you would think teachers would celebrate, yes? No. Both teachers and peers act as gatekeepers and suppress the child's achievement. They are not supposed to do well, so even when they do, it is interpreted as another in a series of expected failures. Is it any wonder when children stop trying?

This is not to say that teachers and classmates are actively and consciously trying to set up poor children for failure. This seems highly unlikely, or at least a fairly rare occurrence. Rather, what happens is the result of unintentional prejudice.

> Early environmental influences often contribute to the development of stereotypical thinking in children. When left unchallenged, such thinking becomes automatically activated, making it difficult for newly acquired ideas established through later learning to be integrated at a deeper level. As a result of this process, it becomes possible for an individual to exhibit unintentionally prejudiced behavior, despite believing that he or she actually maintains a nonprejudicial belief system.... [This] conflict between 'early learning' and 'later learning' [is] *unintentional prejudice.* [This] results in greater personal discomfort as the discrepancy between early and later learning increases ... Actively attending to unexpected emotional reactions such as discomfort and guilt is crucial in heightening awareness.[46]

So, while children in the classroom are being taught to be kind and help their neighbor, the subterranean messages of the culture which brand certain people as "losers" keeps whispering in their ear at a more primal level. We've all been hearing these messages since we were born.

This unintentional prejudice certainly underlies much of racial discrimination in America. It can also be seen in the parents of children who are from higher-class backgrounds. These adults perceive working-class students as unmotivated, unintelligent, and more likely to be emotionally disturbed[47]. In a classroom where students come from multiple backgrounds, the children of wealthier parents are hearing these same discriminatory messages, subtly encouraging gate-keeping behaviors in the classroom which reinforce that lower-class kids should fail as expected.

Along with class-based discrimination, intentional or otherwise, is gender-based discrimination. Girls are subject to numerous biases in the classroom. Surprisingly, even when teachers are observed and told specifically that they are being observed for evidence of gender bias in their teaching, they still unconsciously enact discriminatory practices. Research repeatedly finds numerous instances of such bias:

Boys are …

- 5 times as likely to receive teachers' attention
- 12 times more likely to speak up in class
- the subject of 3 times as many stories as girls
- the subject of biographies read in class 6 times more than biographies of women
- the center of activities designed by teachers
- recipients of more teacher instruction
- asked abstract, open-ended, and complex questions
- praised for ability when successful; credited with bad luck for failure[48].

A more recent study by Lavy and Schlosser[49] found that mixed-gender classrooms have deleterious effects on females. Classrooms with boys tend to be more boisterous, requiring more time and energy from teachers for classroom management and less time and energy on learning. Boys' disruptive behaviors appear to wear teachers down. Conversely, Lavy and Schlosser found that males benefited from having females in the classroom, as the level of violence and disruption was lower.

These findings suggest that the standards for classroom management and successful academic performance are relentlessly male; females are deprived of equal attention and equal teacher resources from very early on in school.

Few areas have been identified in which the abilities of girls are clearly and consistently different from those of boys; and these results may be explained by expectations or socialization or a combination of both, rather than by biological differences[50].

Lower-class children learn powerful gender schema which is particularly rigid from Kindergarten through the fourth grade[51]. They hold gendered occupational stereotypes even at the second grade level, as evidenced by girls predicting future careers for themselves as nurses, and boys as policemen[52]. Although these gender schema become somewhat more flexible in late childhood, lasting effects may be observed into adulthood, as will be discussed further on.

The classroom emphasis for all working-class children is conformity to codes of conduct[53]. You are to stay in your seat, and speak only when spoken to. Raise your hand. You must ask to go to the bathroom. Be quiet. Don't. Don't.

Adolescence: Middle school through high school

Mary Pipher insists that something very odd happens to girls in early adolescence, akin to planes disappearing in the Bermuda Triangle. Their IQ scores drop, as do their scores in math and science[54]. Their assertiveness, playfulness, honesty, and resiliency turn into self-criticism, deference to males, submission, and pessimism as they stop exploring their own interests and conform to society's demand that they display a greater interest in others[55]. Pipher describes this as a split between the authentic or true self of the girl, and a society-driven false self which is required of females in our culture. Cultural standards of beauty and femininity (such as extreme thinness and submissiveness) often run contrary to healthy human development, and adolescence is the time when girls become most vulnerable to these pressures to conform.

Pipher says that bright and sensitive girls are the most vulnerable to culturally-inflicted harm because they pick up the culture's ambivalence about women through sexist media portrayals and other propaganda sources, when they have not yet built the emotional, social, and cognitive skills necessary for effective resistance nor proactivity on their own behalf. It logically follows that bright girls from the lower social classes are doubly vulnerable, as they come to understand the culture's devaluation of both females and the poor.

Language differences persist in junior high and high school. Not only are social class variations in vocabulary and communication styles apparent, but language becomes more highly differentiated by gender. Young women learn to use speech for developing and maintaining relationships, and are typically polite, tentative, and deferential[56]. Young men are more likely to be assertive in dialog, to control the conversation, to interrupt other speakers, and to give problem-solving solutions even when they are not invited[57]. The language or dialect of one's subculture or speech community combines with gender differences in language to form part of one's identity. This particular feature becomes more solidified during the adolescent years.

In adolescence, identity builds upon a teen's location in a social network of family and friends; that is, teenagers' sense of identity is based upon others[58]. In the junior high and high school years, students' social class identity comes not so much from a real knowledge of the class-based segregation of society, but more from the groups or individuals with whom they regularly associate in school—their peers. In essence, adolescents seem to be saying, "Who I am depends on who you believe or want me to be." Thus, peers are given a great deal of power in defining each others' identities.

The role of lower-class adolescents' parents is problematic as well. Specifically, they may value school as a vehicle for social mobility, or they may recall it as a location for their own painful experiences of humiliation and failure[59]. Further, in the parents' own experience the value of school knowledge is questionable. Thus, lower-class adolescents are likely to receive mixed messages from their parents about schooling. These conflicting views then may be reflected in the student's reduced motivation for performance in school.

If there is any confusion in their mind about what their parents expect from them, however, the school makes it clear through tracking that what is expected of lower-class youth is conformity to codes of conduct, and not necessarily educational excellence[60]. "The ritual of tracking informs students of their comparative worth and of the stratified nature of society"[61]. The admirable intention of educational segregation—tracking—is for the benefit of all students, to group students by ability in order to provide the best possible educational experience for each group. However, both the process and outcomes are flawed when criteria other than ability are used to sort students from lower social-class backgrounds.

In the introductory chapter to this book you read about the experiences of several women who experienced the backlash, if you will, of teachers and counselors against youth from lower social-class backgrounds who demonstrated the potential for high achievement. For example, Karen, who came from a farming family, was not expecting to do well because of her family's occupation and socioeconomic status. Here are some additional life stories.

Maggie shared with me her story: "My mother dropped out of high school … [and was later divorced] … so I was raised by my mom whose goal for her daughters was to graduate from high school and have a vocational skill to fall back on. My goal was to become a teacher but high school counselors were determined to keep me on a vocational track. Every semester I fought my way out of dummy English and into college prep classes[62]". Maggie currently works in a university department which focuses on assisting low income and first-generation college students and preparing them for advanced study. She added, "I am still hearing the same kinds of stories from my students today. The bad news is that after 30 years, high school counselors are still denying access."

Another issue that comes up is the knowledge base of the parents regarding tracking and college preparation. Susan said, "You were tracked not only according to your aptitude tests, but also your socioeconomic status. Some of the kids from more affluent neighborhoods, were all in AP [Advanced Placement] classes, honors classes, and I had to fight to get into some of those classes. My parents would not go and make a big stink, maybe some of the other parents who had gone to college, they would go in and say, 'I want my kid in an honors class.' I had to go and say, 'Look, I'm doing very well. I want to be in honors biology.' I would kind of have to advocate for myself[63]". Clearly, not all students would advocate for themselves without any adult support, as this one did.

The underlying biases in grouping practices (such as biased tests and teacher's perceptions based on social class origins) result in striking homogeneity of language, experience, status, and resources[64]. Inevitably, this social reproduction practice excludes bright lower-class children or loses them to learned mediocrity. The school environment thus limits development by establishing what outcomes are valued, and who shall be selected to receive the resources necessary to achieve those outcomes[65].

In a study of 40 low-income and 34 high-income students in one heterogeneous community, Brantlinger found that only 40% of the low-income students felt that teachers liked them, and only 20% felt that teachers cared about them personally[66]. Conversely, 90% of the high-income students felt that teachers liked them[67]. In assessing each other, students perceived intelligence via language usage; that is, the use of "sophisticated" talk was a sign of intelligence[68]. One insightful student said, "The way they talk depends on the status of their parents"[69]. Unintelligent students were described by high-income students as *poor*—"They talk like country people"[70].

The students in Brantlinger's study themselves formed (or inherited) perceptions of each other's characteristics which influenced their social interactions. Specifically, high-income students described low-income students as angry, tough, aggressive, rude, troublemakers; interestingly, they had difficulty pointing to any specific examples to substantiate their perceptions[71]. This echoes earlier negative perceptions of lower-class children by upper-class parents. In adulthood, there is little change from these negative views: lower-class women are perceived by other adults as being primitive, confused, dirty, hostile, inconsiderate, and irresponsible[72]. This underscores lower-class youths' developing class consciousness. They see more clearly how the working class is demeaned and devalued, and they are often unable to cope with this.

In reflecting on how social relationships were influenced by social class, Shelley said, "As I got closer to sixth grade, I could see where things were becoming more stratified in terms of who could be friends with whom. I got more and more worried about these sort of arbitrary, or maybe not so arbitrary, but these lines that were dividing certain people into certain cliques[73]".

Peers exert substantial influence in encouraging or discouraging educational achievement[74]. Sixty-five percent of low-income youth in Brantlinger's study *wanted* to attend college; however, only 35% actually *expected* to attend[75]. A majority of these low-income students did not have a clear understanding of the requirements for college attendance, either in terms of academic standards for admission nor for finances. Of the 15% who did have a clear conception of such requirements, none had rational plans for achieving those requirements[76]. In addition, students of lower socioeconomic origins tend to enroll in the less advantaged tracks in high school[77] in the rare circumstance when they have a choice, thus reducing the probability of acceptance at a selective institution of higher education.

School personnel (teachers, counselors) had not provided information on college, vocational training, nor job-seeking for the low-income students in Brantlinger's study. This may be interpreted as a clear example of what is called "institutionalized allocation," in which representatives of the institution—school—determine who is appropriate for certain social roles—college—and who is not[78]. Low-income students apparently do not generally appear to be college material to teachers and school counselors[79]. Like the leaky pipeline, another apt metaphor is that of "tournament mobility" as described by Rosenbaum[80], wherein those who "lose" the game lose forever; only those who are permitted or encouraged to go on have an opportunity to compete at the next higher level. The choices that adolescents make—and that significant adults make for them—occur at a developmental stage when the consequences of such choices are far-reaching and sometimes irreversible.

Unfortunately, low-income families have few resources to assist in terms of providing useful information to their children about college or careers[81]. Most low-income students in the Brantlinger study had not discussed the possibility of college attendance with their parents; further, only 22% of low-income parents really expected their child to go to college[82]. Most low-income youth in Brantlinger's study had unrealistic or vague post-high school plans, and no matter what their plan, most of the teens felt they would not achieve it.

Penny's experience, shared in the introductory chapter, underscores this problem. She reported receiving little or no guidance in her high school years when she wanted to be assisted in learning about how to get to college. She reported being treated kindly, but was gently steered into secretarial courses while her more advantaged peers received guidance from parents and school personnel towards college. Her ignorance about college caused a cycle in which she did not know what questions to ask and thus was not provided the information she needed to make informed choices about college.

Patrice's experience of seeking information about college echoes this: "The whole process is like walking through a dense forest at dusk, if you don't have some parent or mentor or guide who can help you through the academic maze[83]".

A multitude of forces in the adolescent years conspire to further constrict lower-class young women's development. The attitudes and gender-bound rules developed earlier in life continue, and are reinforced by school personnel. Like many other interviewees, Susan's encounters with high school guidance personnel were not optimal. "I don't think the person really had a clue as to what might be good for me. I remember she was kind of pushing me to become a nurse, and I was never really interested in nursing[84]". In terms of considering college options, she said that guidance was lacking there as well: "I applied to one college, a local college. I got accepted and that was it."

The perspectives of important others about females and about lower social classes become increasingly rigid and negative at the same time when these others' opinions are central to the development of the adolescent's identity. Classroom achievement becomes less likely, even for the brightest lower-class students. A world of possibilities and options from which to choose seems increasingly less probable.

College years

For the students from lower social-class backgrounds who do go to college, it is often the first time that the social class divide becomes strikingly apparent. It is no longer an abstract "out there" concept, but a deeply meaningful personal encounter.

The focus group participants discussed their recollections of going to college for the first time. They reported their initial adjustments to the new and different environs of college. They also recalled the college years as ones of financial duress in which they worked a considerable amount in order to keep themselves in college, even with financial aid awards.

The intelligence and independence of students from lower social-class backgrounds who attend college are necessary for their survival in college. Having had limited prior exposure to other cultural and social class groups, many, like Pam, reported culture clashes as soon as they arrive on campus:

> [In my family] we had always eaten our cereal in the morning, and we always just drank our milk out of the bowl. And you don't know anyone except your roommate [who was a Jewish girl from Long Island], and we're eating breakfast the second day we're there. And so I ate my cereal, and drank my milk, and this one roommate looked at me, and she was clearly of another class, although I didn't know that at the time. And she says [here Pam imitated an accent], 'Oh, you have got to be kidding me.' And she just looked at me with such [disgust]. I had no idea that people just didn't do that. But for her I think that was a real sign of my class.[85]

Pam's experience at a private university was not unique. Some of the respondents' stunned reactions to college, however, had to do with the sheer volume of large university campuses which had not been part of these young women's experiences. Charlene reported, "I walked into some of my first classes, and there were 250-300 people, and I didn't make it!"[86] She dropped out of that school after one semester, leaving behind her national merit scholarship. The size was intimidating; she added, "It was huge and just frightening." She found greater comfort the following year at a smaller state university nearer her home.

College finances were clearly an issue for all the focus group participants. All of the women I interviewed had to work to support themselves and to pay their tuition for college. Jennifer wistfully recalled, "I missed out a lot on the fun part and the traditional college years for other people. I mean, I went to school full-time, I worked full-time. I always did that ... I didn't have a lot of friends, go to a lot of parties, I didn't have that, where other people do[87]". Jennifer went to school with students of greater financial means, who were able to devote themselves solely to their studies and their social lives. Narratives in the next chapter will further illustrate the relationship between social class and financial problems in college.

Given the statistics on the percentage of people in America who complete undergraduate degrees, it seems obvious that the proportion completing graduate degrees would be far less. For many students from lower social-class backgrounds who earn a four-year degree, this achievement is enough. For others, it is just the beginning. This was the case with the women I interviewed.

The choice to pursue an advanced degree is often not understood nor supported by family and friends. Rita recalled the reaction of her family to her declaration that she was going to do just that: "[They said,] 'Why a master's? You already achieved a bachelors. What more do you want?' It was senseless in their eyes. Then when I did a Ph.D., 'Yeah, but didn't you have enough already?'[88]".

Families often present mixed messages to these individuals. They are proud, yet bitter; they are angry, yet loving. For the struggling student, this is confusing and very stressful. The lack of belonging and increasingly strained relations with friends and family can make for a very lonely life. It is no wonder that, at this point for many, the leaky pipeline comes to an end. These students, at various ages, opt out of the higher education system, sometimes returning to homes and traditional expectations in terms of jobs and lifestyles. So these talented people leave the high road and may not realize their potential for achievement, not just in school, but in life. They return to the position of servant, having failed at the road to mastery.

PART III

Real people, huge
obstacles, amazing
achievements

5

Who are we? Voices of working-class women

Who are the unusual women who began their lives as working-class girls, and became women faculty and administrators in colleges and universities in the United States? In this chapter, you will get a glimpse of six women who shared their personal and professional stories with me and with each other in a group interview format. Their perceptions of their own lives provide reflections on being women and being from a lower social class as they completed school, went to college, navigated personal relationships, and more.

In order to gather baseline information about the experiences of women from blue-collar backgrounds who have become faculty and administrators in higher education, a group interview was held. The resulting conversation provided information about both the subtleties of individual experience, as well as patterns across cases within that group. Themes from previous research were confirmed, and new paths of investigation arose.

In the group interview, we discussed experiences related to social class background and professional positions in academe. The participants represented institutions from across the country, as well as across the hierarchy of institutions: community colleges, public universities, private colleges and universities. They were faculty members and administrators, artists and engineers, relatively new/ young professionals and established department heads. In short, a good cross-section was represented.

Our discussion ranged from the material conditions of youth, or what Bourdieu referred to ask "conditions of existence,"[89] to the interpersonal and professional relationships of today. Some of these areas are discussed in further detail in the biographical sketches and in the presentation of themes which are included in later chapters in this book; others are presented here as background information.

Growing Up in Blue-Collar America

The focus group participants conveyed their perceptions of the unique features of growing up in blue-collar families in blue-collar neighborhoods and towns. Their recollections bore on the physical surroundings of home, and the importance of work and education as demonstrated or described by their parents. They vividly described the settings in which they grew up.

Nancy recalled, "Whenever I tell people I'm from Connecticut, I always feel like it's a lie … I go so far as to say, 'No, not the Connecticut you're thinking of. No, we don't have horses, we have factories.'" These women lived in working-class communities in their youth, rural or city neighborhoods, farm or factory based. These communities were fairly homogeneous: "Even the people who we thought were snobby and wealthy, were not, comparatively speaking," said Pam. She added, "I grew up in a town where people had dirt floors."

Two of the respondents related experiences of living on "welfare"; two others recalled times when the family "lost the business, we lost our house" (Eileen); all recalled lives of financial exigency. Linda said, "I didn't ever buy clothes; I always had hand-me-downs. Cousins would come over with the bags, and oh, the shaming! It was heavy duty." If their parents owned a home, it was typically small, filled with children and sometimes extended family. As noted previously, Eileen recalled, "I grew up with a furnace in the living room. The wallpaper was Owens-Corning fiberglass insulation. That was my wallpaper." Comments such as these were followed by knowing nods around the room.

The participants reflected on the values of work and education which their parents modeled (the former) or encouraged (the latter). The overriding message was that education was a way to better your life. Embedded in this message, however, was conflict. Linda recalled that her father worked upwards of 12 hours a day in a liquor store, six or seven days a week. "My father said, 'You don't want to do what I'm doing.' You see, he kept devaluing it." Charlene concurred, noting that her father always said "I was going to have a better life than he had."

While education was promoted, Linda's parents focused their encouragement of education on the boys in the family; "well, mainly my brothers. I wasn't supposed to go to school. I wasn't supposed to end up as an administrator." Gender discrimination was not simply "out there" in the larger culture, it was pervasive in the basic social unit of our culture: the family.

Schooling from Kindergarten through High School

The women discussed their recollections of educational experiences from Kindergarten through high school, and many commonalities appeared. They recalled being high achievers at an early age, demonstrating academic excellence. Their encounters with school personnel demonstrated the participants' mixed perceptions of designated helping professionals and educators. Teachers, administrators, and counselors sometimes noticed the respondents' budding talents and encouraged their achievement, but more frequently the respondents remembered inattention or active discouragement from these school professionals. According to their stories, these negative practices were sometimes based on gender discrimination, but also appeared in tracking practices which seemed to have been based on social class rather than ability. The women also often reported that they felt like outsiders in their school settings. These school-related findings are illustrated with specific stories from their lives.

All of the women said, in one way or another, what Nancy said, "I was a smart kid." They were outstanding performers in academics from early on, and typically graduated at or near the top of their classes. Some recalled encouragement and attention from teachers, while others recalled negative notice from school personnel. Even for one of the youngest members of the focus group, gender roles were the backdrop for thinking about options after high school: "... that limited view, Mr. ___ had. He was very sexist in his approach to counseling students ... [if I had done what he wanted] I would have been a secretary..... [if you were female] in high school you had to take the secretarial track."

Although many of the respondents recalled expressing higher aspirations to teachers, counselors, and administrators, if they received any advice from school personnel, it was to pursue traditional female occupations: nurse, teacher, or secretary. Only one participant recalled positive interactions with a school counselor when her mother declined to support her college aspiration:

> Mrs. _____ helped me out when I came to a dilemma with speaking with my mom about going to school, and my mother said, 'Well you know, your brothers will have to support a family.' And I was just blown away. And I just remember going to see Mrs. ____, and she said, 'Now, you have just as much right to a career as anybody else.' (Eileen)

A few participants mentioned the practice of tracking in their schools. The stories they related seemed to indicate two parallel tracking processes: one based on academic performance, and one based on social class. These sometimes came in conflict. Pam noticed a disparity in student treatment in her small homogeneous town based on parents' occupation: "The kids whose parents were either teachers or administrators in the high schools were kind of a class above the rest of us." Nancy recalled being placed in a group of smart, affluent students in her larger school district, "but when it came time to give out awards at the end of the year, apply for fairly prestigious scholarships in the town, [I was] shut out completely." When asked who was responsible for her exclusion, she answered, "I can only assume, teachers and guidance counselors."

A recurrent theme expressed during the course of the conversation was that of feeling like an outsider. At least twenty times a sentiment was voiced such as, "I never fit really anywhere ..." (Charlene). This sense of other-ness, as they voiced it, often had to do with being smart, and thus different, at school and sometimes at home. It sometimes had to do with excellence in athletics, with sexual orientation, with exceptional performance in mathematics or science, or with personality: "I'm a stubborn SOB!" (Charlene). Sometimes the outsider status was based on social class background; Linda recalled her parents' attempts to socialize with families of a higher status in her small city, throwing her together with children with whom she had little in common. "I never could relate, and they always had [nicer] clothes and I was always jealous.... It was pretty much a lonely childhood ..."

Being an outsider had a positive aspect, however; the interviewees reported acting independently and assertively, particularly in the school setting. It was necessary for them to advocate for themselves, because their parents did not have enough experience with education themselves to advocate for their children. Another asset, as Nancy said, "I can relate well to people. I understand differentness ..." She added, "I was an anomaly in my family, but one that they were really supportive of ... I felt really loved and accepted despite how different I was from the other people in my family."

The College Experience

As noted in the previous chapter, for first-generation college students, entering college for the first time was a cross-cultural awakening of sorts. Their encounters ranged from the ridiculous to the sublime, but certainly required significant external and internal adjustments to this strange new world. In chapter 4 you read about Pam's "cereal bowl" encounter as an example of culture clashes with upper-class roommates. Students dealt with harsh financial realities as well. Pam also shared this memory:

> I had a very wealthy roommate at that point. She drove a Porsche, had a separate wardrobe moved into her half of the room to hold her shoes, OK? … I'm on work-study, trying to get partial scholarships so that I can do my laundry, take the bus to class, on the $20 my grandmother would send me in the mail. It was a challenge. And so I walk in, and she's on the phone with her father, saying 'Daddy, $350 a month just isn't enough.' Of like pocket money. And I was like, it's not? [laughter] I couldn't even understand what she was talking about, really. At the time, it was almost a non-occurrence. Because there was not a thing in me that could relate to that. $350 is a lot, you know?

These individuals had to work, often and hard, just to stay in college. Charlene recalled all the odd jobs she did to make money: selling newspapers, working at the coffee shop, working for her father [who delivered newspapers]. She remembers thinking, "Well, if I was going to go to college and I was going to survive, I had to work all these jobs…. I thought everybody worked like that."

Professional Life

The focus group interview revealed the participants' perceptions regarding their professional lives in academe. They noted the difficulty of reconciling their blue-collar work ethic with an upper-class work environment and upper-class colleagues. They voiced continuing concerns about job security and financial security. The women discussed their sense of not fitting in the professional environment of higher education. This sense of other-ness appeared to be based, in part, on differing class-based realities between themselves and their colleagues who came from higher social classes. The women recounted stories of changing superficial attributes such as attire and language style to meet the surface norms of higher education; referring to this as being a "chameleon." In addition, as they reported seeing it, their academic and subsequent professional success in higher education was paired with a distancing from family and hometown friends who did not understand the daily life and work of a higher education professional. These interwoven topics are discussed below.

The social class backgrounds of these women clearly had an impact on their current professional lives. Responding to the work ethic modeled for them by their parents, they worked long and hard. Given the nature of their work, this was often a painful and costly effort.

> ... coming from a working-class background, I try to fit my work now into that work ethic. And it's impossible ... No matter how hard you work in this field, the work isn't done. You don't have a stack of something to show for it, bricks or roads, or—my dad worked roads—and this profession could just kill me, in my effort to try to get it to fit that work ethic. (Pam)

Nancy said, "I find that my work values don't match most of my colleagues' work values." She has seen them work fewer hours than she, and put less effort into the work in general. "Someone is paying you to do this job. If you're not doing the work that you say you're going to do, you're stealing. That's wrong." Her colleagues in the room concurred. She added, "They have often, it seems to me, the luxury of more freedom to make those calls for themselves. Privilege, I guess." Linda expanded on the issue of work ethics, and spoke resentfully about her 9-to-5 colleagues who called her a "workaholic." She explained, "I don't consider it an addiction to work, I just see it as a value system that, you do it right or you don't do it at all. That was drilled into me."

A related matter focused on job security, and underlying concerns about financial matters. Nancy said that her social class background "makes me feel more vulnerable. I think that privileged people assume that they'll always have jobs. And I don't, at all. I feel really lucky to have a job." She continued, "I feel very conscious of the fact that that job could disappear. I take it really seriously when there's budget cutting and down-sizing." She described a recent situation in which faculty from higher social class backgrounds clearly did not have these feelings of vulnerability. While one faculty member from a background similar to hers "totally comes unglued" at the mention of budget cuts, she says the others paid no attention. "It never even comes up. [They say] 'Well, of course you're going to have a job, no big deal, something else will come along.'" She suspected that downsizing was not stressful for them in that they have always had a financial buffer; i.e., there was family money or somebody they are connected with who can float them through such times or who can make the important social connections that translate into advantages in securing a new position.

The theme of "not fitting" which began at home and school for these women continued for them in the professional environment. Charlene noted, "Many of my colleagues at the college that I taught at were from fairly wealthy families ... they had gone to places like MIT and Harvard." She added, "I just didn't fit with these folks. We did work together as colleagues, but we just never had any sort of intimate relationships." Charlene noted that her work-related friendships were most often with clerical staff members, who were more likely to come from backgrounds similar to hers. She said of her more advantaged colleagues, "My reality is so different from their reality. My reality is of a father who grew up on welfare, who worked from the age of 15 doing the same job, and that was not who my colleagues were."

Pam thoughtfully commented on the class realizations she had come to regarding her professional experiences. In reflecting on the stories she had shared with us in connection with her socioeconomic background, such as the one about drinking milk from her cereal bowl, and which she had shared with colleagues in the workplace, she said:

> There seems to be some judgment that comes with that. Like yes, your story is different than their story, .. But for those folks who fall higher than me, socioeconomically, they approach those conversations, the hearing of my story, with some judgment. That doesn't always feel really good, I think, socially.

This sense of being negatively judged based on social class background, as opposed to social class as a neutral fact, was an undercurrent which surfaced throughout the interviews. However, the focus group participants found many advantages to having come from blue-collar backgrounds and working in higher education. These included a knowledge of how to function on a small budget, how to relate to many different kinds of people (especially valuable with a diverse student body), a first-hand knowledge of persistence in the face of considerable obstacles, and an ability (perhaps more gender related) to balance many things at one time. Linda summed up her experience as "survival of the fittest," referring to both her youth and her professional life.

In reference to the workplace, participants discussed how they had overcome the problem of not fitting in. We discussed many seemingly superficial attributes, such as attire and dialect, which these women modified to match prevailing norms in the social atmosphere. In our discussion, the word "chameleon" was used many times to describe the process of changing outer form in order to maximize the comfort level of self and others. Nancy thoughtfully suggested, "I think we're non-threatening [to others]." However, the disguise sometimes slips: Pam noted, "I still say 'workin'' instead of 'working' [laughter]." Eileen added, "I still have 'bre-fess', I don't have 'breakfast'." Discussing the topic of professional attire, and shopping at Talbots (a women's-wear store known for a certain New England flair associated with private schooling), Charlene said, "I still haven't figured that game out," to which Pam responded, "I just figured that out this year [laughs]." This "chameleon" phenomenon represents a major theme which is covered in greater depth later in this book.

The focus group participants also reflected on differences between the institutions in which they worked, and how they felt they fit in or did not fit into that particular rank of institution (in terms of prestige or exclusivity). Charlene spoke of her choice of her current professional position:

> Why did I choose the community colleges? Because we take care of the working poor. That's who our clientele is, that's who our students are.... there's not the prestige, and I really don't care there's not the prestige.

To this Pam responded, "It almost feels like shaming, sometimes. Like that, you should feel ashamed." This comment was followed by thoughtful silence in the room, and nods of agreement. Another participant from a top-tier institution concurred that this was an accurate assessment of the hierarchical climate among higher education institutions.

Charlene also questioned the motives of some top administrators who chose to work in the community college, most of whom come from higher social class backgrounds. "Mostly because the pay is so good, not because of the mission, they're there because of the pay."

The professional lives and successes of these women also reminded them of the distance that had grown between them and their families of origin, as well as from old home-town friends. Charlene said, "I know there are certain things that I cannot say with my family because ..." Nancy finished the sentence for her: "They won't understand." That blue-collar individuals do not understand the daily work of academic professionals was an understatement. This cross-cultural fact created a chasm which these women have come to accept with resignation. This important theme will be addressed in greater depth later in this book as well.

6

Their words, their lives

This chapter includes biographical sketches of the women I interviewed individually. I was fortunate to spend a few hours with each woman. I essentially asked each one to tell me the story of their life. These profiles provide descriptive details, as well as hinting at some of the major life themes and key transitions which emerged in the course of our interview. Some of these themes become evident as patterns across cases.

Pat

Pat immediately struck me as a no-nonsense person. As a faculty member in the social sciences, she was particularly interested in the topic of my study and approached me very directly about it. Pat came from a small working-class community in the northwestern part of the country, where her father worked as a boilermaker for the railroad. Her mother was a homemaker who also kept the books for small entrepreneurial ventures (such as garbage collection) which the family conducted on the side to help generate income.

Pat's talents were apparent at an early age, both academically and artistically, and were encouraged by her parents. Like many other respondents, she said, "There was never any doubt that I was going to be the smart one [in the family]." In a town which was relatively isolated and homogeneous, a few female teachers noticed her intellectual curiosity and encouraged it with individual time and even personal gifts. Her mother was the focal point in terms of college planning; even while she was dying of cancer, she took Pat to visit colleges.

Pat's college years stretched to college decades, as she needed to work in order to pay for tuition. She says, "... a great portion of my adult life has been [paying] tuition every term." Her work varied from bartending to academic administration and college teaching as she completed first a baccalaureate degree and finally a doctorate. At age 50, she is currently employed in a tenure-track faculty position in the social sciences at a community college. She is a single parent of a preadolescent son, which has had an impact on her educational and career choices as well.

Upon the death of Pat's mother, prior to Pat's senior year of high school, Pat's father began drinking heavily and ceased to be a source of financial or emotional support for Pat. Rather, her family ties became defined in terms of their demands on her and their need for her support. Ironically, while her siblings do not have the higher education credentials which Pat has, and have instead chosen working-class jobs and more traditional gender roles, she perceived their lifestyles as more comfortable and financially secure. Because of the continuous financial drain of higher education, combined with single parenting and limited income in her professional positions, she said, "I'm the only one of the three that has a working class income. I'm still making under $40,000 a year." She estimated her siblings' (and spouses') combined incomes to be more than double that.

An overarching theme in Pat's life, like that of many other respondents, was that of the loner, the outsider. "I'm the odd one," Pat noted, as she described her early identification in the family as "the smart one." That marginalized identity continued during her years of college study and professional work: "I was the only woman for so long. We finally have one other woman in the ___ Department after all these years." This sense of marginality was not simply intellectually based or gender based, however; there were distinct social class overtones: "... some of that is class. I would say most of the men that I work with in the department are middle class people [from] professional backgrounds. Their parents were educated, in other words." Pat's peripheral status was one that she had come to accept. She said, "I got comfortable being the outsider, the person on the fringe, the one that doesn't fit in.... You just sort of get comfortable as the odd guy out."

Jennifer

Jennifer is a young community college professional whose educational and career paths have been non-linear, as the respondents often reported. She has never known her biological father, and described her mother as "a partier." Her stepfather, who joined her life when she was a pre-schooler, has always been an entry-level postal service employee. Jennifer's mother has always been employed in clerical jobs, and disliked her work.

Although Jennifer was an outstanding student in school, her talents were unacknowledged by her family. Recalling both her shyness and her exceptional achievement in junior high school, she said, "I got hundreds in my four basic subjects.... I was embarrassed because we had an assembly and [I] had to go get these awards." Similar to other respondents, she did not recall ever being advised by school personnel to take college preparatory courses in high school, nor was she encouraged to consider going to college, regardless of her early academic excellence. She recalled, "… as far as actually encouraging me personally, no, definitely a lack of that looking back…. no, no one ever said much about college, or really encouraged me, or sat down and said, look at all the choices you have."

After graduating from high school a semester early, Jennifer worked for a year at odd jobs such as baby-sitting. She decided to attend a community college when her then-boyfriend decided to go, and encouraged her to try it. (He quit; she stayed.) When asked how she decided upon a major, it was again without guidance. When she went to the campus to sign up for courses, she was asked to determine a major right away. "I had no direction and no one to sit down with me…. [The admissions officer] said, 'Pick a major, here you go, just pick.'"

Jennifer "just picked" business, completed her associate's degree, and continued directly to baccalaureate studies. Like many other respondents, work was not an option, but a necessity which began in the teen years and continued in the college years. However, there was a cost in terms of a social life. As noted in a previous chapter, Jennifer talked about the necessity of working full-time while attending college full-time, which precluded the social life and participation in activities which are typically part of a collegiate experience. She clearly missed having the time to socialize and form close college friendships.

Jennifer completed her master's degree in business, and then sallied forth into what she believed would be an economically promising and secure future. However, what she encountered was a combination of gender discrimination, age discrimination, and other factors. At age 28, Jennifer is a slender, attractive young woman who might have had a career in modeling. She described her difficulty in finding suitable employment: "I was told several times by men, especially older men, to not say I had a master's degree. Not put that on my resume." People told her, "You're overqualified, you're too intimidating." One prospective employer told a mutual friend, "We can't hire her, she's got a master's degree, we only have bachelor's …" She struggled through two difficult years of job-seeking by cocktail waitressing, and finally broke into her first professional position, her current position as an entry-level financial administrator in a community college. However, her struggles were not over. Jennifer described a recent situation in which she was meeting with a professional colleague regarding budget matters, "… and he looks at me and says, 'what color lipstick is that?' and I thought, oh no …"

The intimidation she mentioned earlier is also something which Jennifer has considered as a factor in her social life. Specifically, her romantic relationships with working-class men have suffered because of her advanced level of education: "In a couple of relationships the guys made comments [like], 'You think you're better than me.' … I don't think he could accept the fact that I [attended college] and that was definitely a problem."

Sharon

Sharon is a tenured faculty member in a premiere research university. Seeing her on that day, in a sunlit office filled with books, it was difficult to believe that she had to leave home without graduating from high school because at age 15 her parents refused to allow her to eat at home any longer if she did not pay room and board. Sharon's father was a boxcar checker for the railroad in a large city, and her mother was a homemaker. This family of eight lived in a working-class ethnic neighborhood which was heavily influenced by religion.

Sharon was identified as "smart" very early on in school; she was also assertive and advocated for herself. As a sophomore in a parochial school, she decided to apply to a public magnet school where she believed she would benefit from a higher quality of education, including college preparatory courses. She was accepted, and with her attendance, her exposure to a more heterogeneous population and adoption of new values was troubling to her parents and her church. "There were a lot of conflicts about friendships I had with young black women. I invited one over once, and my parents made me call her up and tell her she couldn't come." Concerns over issues of equality, in terms of race, ethnicity, and gender, were common in the women I interviewed. Their sensitivity to "outsider" status appeared as concern over the marginality of specific others and the subsequent mistreatment of women, non-whites, and other groups branded as "different" and thus normatively deviant.

Unlike many other respondents, Sharon was encouraged to achieve and singled out for attention from teachers from early on. She described a scenario in which a nun placed her in charge of the classroom for an extended period of time at the age of eight. She was selected as a lab assistant for a high school chemistry teacher.

Sharon had been identified at home as "the smart one.… I was going to be the first person to go to college in this family.… You could be anything you want." Yet at the same time, there were conflicting messages: "My father would say it wasn't right for women to be taking jobs away from men. And I would argue with him."

Serendipitously, as family tensions were rising, Sharon was selected for an academic summer camp for gifted high school juniors. This became a key transitional point for her, as she came in contact with faculty members at a prestigious university who recognized her talent, were shocked at the severity of her treatment at home, and encouraged her to apply for early admission to the university. Sharon recalled that her parents felt threatened by her foray into this foreign (academic) environment. "Suddenly, I was being drawn away, and that was how I got the order to pay rent or move out, because my intellectual work wasn't doing anything for them. I wasn't of any value to them, unless I was working." With the help of a school social worker, Sharon got on the school lunch program, and then moved into foster care. In January of her senior high-school year she left school for the university, without having graduated from high school, but with substantial scholarship aid and the promise of a better life, in many ways.

Sharon's college years were relatively smooth and uneventful, her way strewn with academic honors, and she continued directly through the Ph.D. at an Ivy League university with full fellowship awards. Her first professional position was as a junior faculty member at that institution, and then she returned to the university which had first welcomed her as a student, where she remains today as a tenured faculty member. At the Ivy League institution where she earned the Ph.D., she noticed both gender and social class differences: "It's a boys' club. An upper class boys' club.... My sense is that everybody at [Ivy] is from middle and upper class. Very rarely do you meet any students from lower class backgrounds, but certainly among the faculty, there were not people who had come from the lower class." She went on to say, "They were professors who were children of other academics, or they were children of businessmen, business/professional class people, they were really upper class types. You know, the ones with the pedigrees."

Sharon went through a rough period of re-evaluating her own views and values when she got divorced a few years ago. At the time of our interview, she was 42 years old, and had a young child. She wondered if her success in academe had anything to do with the demise of her marriage. Her ex-husband was an abuser; he was also from a higher social class background. She acknowledged one of her own stereotypes of such men: "I had made the grave mistake of thinking that because I had married upward, class wise, that I was not going to be subject to the kind of abuse I had seen my mother subject to.... I married a man who was an [Ivy League] undergraduate, and I knew his parents were economists. His father was [a high ranking political official], and they were well educated, and yet the same thing happened."

This type of class-based stereotyping, both positive and negative, goes in both directions; that is, not only are negative stereotypes of working-class people held by those in higher social classes, but people from blue-collar backgrounds are equally capable of making baseless positive attributions about those in higher classes. This was a recurring pattern in the interviews.

Stephanie

Stephanie is a young, happily married mother of a toddler, and a new faculty member at a prestigious research university. As an ethnic minority, she was aware of how different her life was from her parents' lives. "We met with an investment counselor … we're buying a home that I don't think my parents could have dreamed about buying. We drive nice cars. My parents never had nice cars." At the same time, Stephanie was concerned about becoming too materialistic. At her current professional location, she has seen colleagues who are "in that whole yuppie mode," buying expensive cars and homes. "I don't want to be that kind of person. I don't want to be pretentious …" This sentiment has carried over into her selection of friends. "There's kind of a snooty thing here at [Ivy], there's a lot that come from tradition and family money. There's an arrogance. The people we seem to click with are people that could care less about that. They are down to earth. They don't have to be wearing the nicest things. They can go to McDonald's just as easily as going to a really nice restaurant." These sentiments were echoed by other respondents as well.

Stephanie's high school years were marred by the breakup of her parents' marriage. Her parents immigrated to this country, her father from Central America and her mother from Europe. Her father's cultural values included extramarital affairs for men; her mother's did not. Stephanie and her two younger sisters were left with a mother who had difficulty coping with single parenting and the financial strain of surviving on a telephone operator's salary. Her father had opposed the divorce and no longer wanted to see any of them. Her mother had a nervous breakdown, lost both the house and the car, and suddenly the parent-child roles were reversed: for her final two years of high school, Stephanie was the parent of the family. "My mother couldn't hold a job for two years. We moved from apartment to apartment … mostly because we got kicked out." She said that her mother would sometimes disappear for a few days at a time. "So I had to make sure that my sister got off to school … talk to people, to not take away things like our appliances, washers and dryers …" She also worked during this time, sometimes "under the table" to help pay the rent and buy food for the family.

The culture clash at home paralleled the clash of social class cultures in her urban public-school experience. After a sterling elementary school experience where she was placed in a program for gifted students, and also skipped a grade, she went to an all-black school for fifth and sixth grade. "Having brown skin ... I always felt very comfortable." She noted that her friends had always complimented her on being "colorblind" because she did not have issues around race and ethnicity. She was then bussed from her working-class neighborhood to junior high and high school in an upper-class neighborhood. In addition to this being "the first time I ever was introduced to any kind of prejudice or racial tensions," there were other contrasts as well. She described one of the differences between her experience and that of her new classmates: "... when kids turned 16, a lot of them got cars.... It was a very different, intimidating environment." She added, "... we were latchkey kids. My mother had to work, and we would come home from school and be on our own.... other kids we went to school with would go to nice camps, and horseback riding ..." In commenting on socioeconomic differences, Stephanie went on, "Sometimes I felt like I wasn't good enough, with peer groups, I didn't have new clothes or new shoes, or couldn't do those kinds of things, and didn't run in those circles."

Stephanie was reflective when it came to the cumulative advantage that accrues to privileged and gifted children, and the cumulative disadvantage of what she called the "underprivileged": "... because I was in the gifted program, I had access to some of the most incredible teachers ... how unfortunate it is, that we set up a system where only the gifted children get access to that. Because these are the people that have a jump ahead anyways."

Stephanie's college choices were very much constrained by the needs of her immediate family, and thus she chose to stay within commuting distance of home, although she initially lived on campus. Her enjoyment of college life was likewise limited due to her considerable responsibilities, both to herself and others. She recalled, "I always had a job. So it was school and work, and I had a boyfriend. That was it." She began as an honors pre-med student, but because of the pressures from so many directions, she did not fare well academically and lost her scholarship. She had to leave school to work full-time to earn enough money to return. She returned, changed her major to psychology, and re-earned her scholarship for the subsequent semesters of her undergraduate years.

Having completed a baccalaureate degree in psychology, Stephanie was motivated to investigate graduate study for the same reason as many of my other respondents: the lack of viable options for employment. She remembered thinking, "OK, what am I going to do with a psych undergraduate degree?" She continued doing secretarial work and retail store sales. She selected a graduate school of business, again, for its location close to home; although by then her mother was stable, had secure employment, and had a new and successful marriage.

Stephanie's path, like others, approximated a zig-zag at this stage. She dropped out of graduate school to get married, switched schools, got divorced, changed specialties, finished an MBA degree, and finally moved back home with her mother and stepfather in order to pursue a doctorate in business. As she said, "It was a really bumpy road." She had a female role model and mentor in her doctoral program who exposed her to higher education as an occupational choice, and who worked with Stephanie to position her for employment in this field; pushing her to conduct important research, publish papers, and otherwise build a winning resume.

With Stephanie's professional success, however, came costs. As someone who saw herself as a "loner" since elementary school, she continued in this role. She said, "I feel this constant sense that, I have to keep proving myself, that I am good enough." Coming from a non-Ivy institution, she reported feeling compared unfavorably with professional colleagues by them: "Now I have to deal with a lot of the faculty who come from Yale and Harvard and Brown and other ivy league schools. 'Oh, well, her Ph.D. is from [non-ivy] University. How good can she really be?'" In addition, Stephanie noticed a gender imbalance: "... and then being female. This [institution] doesn't have very many female faculty." She has felt the pressure to prove herself professionally, while her roles as mother and wife also compete for her time. When these roles have conflicted, the words of her father (with whom she has tenuously reconciled) at last Christmas are recalled: "... 'You haven't served your husband dinner.' ... even though I'm his daughter, I take the back seat from the man ..."

Karen

Karen hailed from the heart of hog-farming country. Her father was a tenant farmer, her mother a homemaker and family manager. She recalled that, "We lived three miles from town, but it was like a million miles.... It was pretty isolated."

Like other respondents, Karen was one of the few from her high school who went "far away" to college; most stayed close to home if they went to college at all. Gender discrimination for Karen, like many other respondents, began at home. Karen described her father several times as "a total and complete sexist." She recalled that "his idea was, everything was for the sons." It was all right for the two girls to do well in school, and to aspire to a college education, but the family resources were focused on the two boys in the family. "My dad's idea was that I would go to college, and then I would marry a farmer, and become a farm wife. That was what I was supposed to do."

As noted previously, Karen remembered her high school teachers being surprised when she was a high achiever; this she attributed to her status as a farmer's daughter. Her school counselor provided no useful information on colleges outside of her state, except one—his information consisted of the knowledge that "they served beer in the student union." She took the initiative to write to Harvard, but they did not accept women at that time and referred her to Radcliffe. However, the pull of family was strong; she chose a school of which her parents approved based on the fact that "it was a day's drive away, so it was OK." (In her rural area, such a distance was considered "far away.") She now regrets this choice, because it was a huge institution: "… it was too big a place, and I got no attention at all…. So it was an easy place to get lost."

Many of Karen's college choices, including choice of a major and career field, were made in an attempt to secure her father's attention and approval. "I figured if I could do something he was interested in, he would be interested in me."

Like other respondents, Karen's college years were marked by academic excellence and hard work. "I didn't have the kind of college experience that most kids have because I was working probably around 30 or 40 hours a week in order to just make it work." At the end of her undergraduate years, the options available seemed to be limited to graduate school, or employment as a secretary. She chose to continue for her Ph.D. in a specialized and quantitative social science field.

In her graduate program, there were five women in a field of 150 students. This male/female ratio continued in her career as a faculty member in a male-dominated specialty. She recalled of her first position, "it was a horrible place to be." Even today as a tenured professor, she noted, "women in [this field] are still unusual. Women in [this field] don't have the same kind of career paths as men do." When asked to identify how her career path has differed from males in the field, she recalled that even in graduate school, she was assigned a "nurturer" role, having students and faculty over for dinner parties and conversation, while male students were encouraged to write articles for publication. "Instead of saying, 'Oh, you ought to be publishing this article,' I would be the one that was recommended to be on the committee." Similarly, in her first role as an assistant professor, males were mentored differently. "I could have probably published a lot more, if that had been what had been valued over and above making the place OK. It's certainly true that some of the people who I would regard as mentors here would have mentored a man differently than they mentored me." Her conclusion was that, rather than considering her career goals, "I was really easy to use, so they used me."

Karen revealed that she had, indeed, married the son of a farmer during the course of graduate school, and had two children. Her husband was abusive, and after more than a decade she divorced him. Her feelings about her husband and her father have overshadowed any objective measurement of her career as successful. "I was never enough of a success to actually succeed in getting the attention from my father, or to make my husband happy. He was never happy."

The divorce was a key transitional time for Karen. She reflected on her personal and professional roles and goals, including her current position as an academic administrator. "I sort of came to the view that, I like this [job]! And it's OK, so I should probably do that. Instead of feeling badly about not being a famous [specialist]." When asked to expand, she said that people in this specialty area "are not really nice people by nature.... They are reasonably arrogant.... Women in [this field] don't do very well." She continued, "They don't typically treat women very well ... they don't expect a woman to do very well." This translates into low expectations, disrespect, poor treatment, and an environment in the specialty which she described as "cutthroat." Ultimately, she has accepted her current place in academe, and not having achieved fame in her field; alluding to the competition and unethical tactics required to achieve fame, she said, "I don't respect the things that you have to do to do that."

Rita

Rita has been fighting one of the biggest battles female academics encounter: tenure combat. A respected researcher and teacher in a state university, Rita has felt unfairly treated in being considered for tenure, but not on the basis of gender nor ethnicity. It has been a more elusive discrimination which she views as profoundly personal and at the same time political.

Rita's parents came from Puerto Rico, her father recruited first to do agricultural labor, and then steel mill labor. Her father had a third-grade education, and her mother a sixth-grade education. Her mother was primarily a homemaker, but also laundered clothes and cooked meals for factory workers in order to help the family financially.

In her family of 5, Rita was the only one to go to college. She ultimately earned a Ph.D. in a social science field. She remembered her early years of schooling as positive. "I was always an achiever. I always did well. I was told I was doing well." During her high school years, however, her father had a nervous breakdown. He went on disability, and decided to return home to Puerto Rico. That was somewhat of a setback for Rita educationally. Classes were conducted in Spanish. "I had to forget English and learn a whole new language."

An advantage of the move to Puerto Rico was that she learned about a new opportunity: college. In the United States, she had not considered college. She recalled that in the steel mill community, students were prepared for work in the steel mill. So, "even though I was a good student, I was never talked to about college." However, when she went to Puerto Rico, "everyone was talking college." A girlfriend told her about the availability of funding. "She said, 'Haven't you heard of grants, scholarships, loans?' I wasn't even informed. So here I had to go to this other country to become informed about the opportunities for college." She recalled further, "It had never, ever, occurred to me to go to college, even though I had good grades. It was just a no-no."

Rita attended college in Puerto Rico, continuing through the Master's level. While finances were tight during her college years, she remembered being easily able to live on a tight budget: "If I had two bucks a week to live on, that was good. That was OK.... Clothing was given to us or me." Her immediate and extended family sacrificed in order to help support her while she completed her B.S. degree. However, like other respondents, the pursuit of advanced degrees was not understood or welcomed by the family. As detailed in chapter 4, Rita's family's patience wore thin when she stated her goal of a graduate degree, and openly stated their opposition. Thus, Rita found herself without family support for that level of study. "It was more isolating, because it was much more difficult [for them] to relate."

Rita was recruited for a position in a United States public school and had been working for three years when she was unexpectedly laid off. This helped her to decide that it was time to pursue the terminal degree. Doctoral programs were not available in Puerto Rico, so Rita chose a U.S. university based on incidental exposure to the program during her earlier studies. She was able to obtain an assistantship based on her dual-minority status as a female Hispanic. She recalls those years of hard work and study as "difficult" and "isolating." A romantic relationship could not survive her dedication to work and study. At the same time, her geographic and emotional distance from family took a toll. "Family was not there. Family wasn't even—it had to be second, instead of first. I wasn't used to that."

Like other respondents, Rita now resents the fact that her doctoral program did not adequately prepare her for the realities of professional academic life. She was never able to teach during her doctoral program, and she has felt that this hurt her. "... in the long run, I was supposed to be a professor. As a teaching assistant, that was the only opportunity I would get to practice those skills or to develop those skills. That's the stuff that you don't really know and they don't tell you." She also wished she had known more about the politics of academia.

As an entry-level faculty member at the state university where she remains today, she said, "I didn't get the right coaching, the right mentoring." She reported feeling that she had gotten mixed messages about what was valued in the institution, and had devoted time to what the institution espoused as a value, and thus had not yet received tenure because it was not the true value of the institution. After ten years of silent compliance with the institution's changing expectations, Rita has been discovering her voice. "I said, 'I will sue.' That's when they heard me for the first time." She now sees her tenure quest as simply "the issue of principle and dignity."

The strain of the past decade has brought into question other areas of Rita's life. She is single, and said with regret, "My biological clock has stopped ticking, just about." In addition, she says, "… working: it just takes up so much of your time and you feel like it's never enough. There's other parts of you that you are not feeding either." Her long work hours have prevented her from having the kind of relationships she expected to have; first, with her family, who live in Puerto Rico, and second, with a lifelong partner and family of her own. She said that her career is "an isolating thing. It can also be intimidating to other people. You're culturally isolated, educationally isolated, professionally isolated." She thought back to her youth and her mother's socialization of her: "She trained me for domestic work. She didn't train me to be an educator or how to deal in the world of professionalism. With a man, you are always geared to become professional."

Marcia

Marcia said she thinks of herself "as a secretary". This was ironic, given that she had earned a Ph.D. in Comparative Literature, and began her career as a faculty member. She was extremely articulate, and her lively intellect was apparent within a few minutes of conversation. At age 54, she has been justifiably angry at the premature termination of her faculty career, which is detailed further in this sketch.

Marcia's father worked at a number of jobs, as a milk delivery man, lathe operator, and house painter; but his permanent calling was to the bottle. Her mother was the reliable supporter of the family and held various jobs in addition to homemaker—factory worker and waitress, for example—but then returned to college, graduating at the same time that Marcia graduated from high school, and working thereafter as a teacher.

Marcia's high school valued athletics, and thus she and her academically-oriented siblings were considered "odd ... I think in those days they called us egg-heads ..." The teachers and administrators did not notice or encourage her talents; as she recalled of school personnel, "No one was interested. No one was terribly impressed.... this was a football high school. I was of no use to them." Unlike other respondents, however, Marcia was encouraged by her school counselor to apply for college scholarships. She did so, and received adequate scholarship awards to attend college.

As a good Catholic, "you were strongly encouraged to attend a Catholic institution." Therefore, she chose the nearest Catholic college. She enjoyed the change in environment, "having conversations with people who were actually interested in books and poetry ... instead of football." She recalled this period of her life with mixed emotions, recalling it as one of emotional difficulty, but one of the few times when "I had a circle of friends who shared many of my interests".

Marcia recalled that the decision to continue on to graduate school was an easy one. Like other respondents, she found herself with the prospect of unemployment based on her major in English Literature. "So, I thought, well, I think I'd better go to graduate school. It was a very haphazard decision." During her college years she worked as a nanny and cleaning houses. She lived frugally on her scholarship funds, "and I was happy and I just read and I wrote, and it was fun." She also recalled that "they tossed me into a classroom" without any preparation for teaching. However, after an initially steep learning curve, she came to enjoy it immensely.

When Marcia was at the ABD (all-but-dissertation) stage, and not progressing with her dissertation, she decided to leave the university and teach, which she did for three years. Upon returning and successfully completing her dissertation, she said, "that was the end of my career." The competition for jobs was fierce across the country. "By finishing my degree, I realized I had actually priced myself out of the market. Everyone was perfectly happy to have me as the lowest rung on the teaching hierarchy at their university, but as soon as they would have to put me on a tenure track, then they suddenly could do quite easily without me." Marcia referred to some research which speaks to the "unspoken policies of higher education" as they pertain to the hiring and firing of young female faculty. "It worked out very neatly that way. It was three years and then it was out."

Marcia reflected upon this with considerable bitterness. "I had gone all the way through all those years of school doing exactly what everyone appeared to want me to do. I made good grades. I was outstanding and industrious and always polite, and what I got for it was eventually a degree which turned me into a hard-core unemployable. For four years after that, I could not get a job doing anything." In understatement, she added, "I found this very annoying and I still do."

Marcia moved back home and found part-time employment as a secretary, which became her primary career and source of income for the next two decades. She also worked as a property manager and had contract work conducting library research for a publisher.

During her early years of career transition, Marcia was able to get adjunct faculty work at a small private college. However, it didn't work out. "The students at [private] college were clearly a different social class from me; and we communicated so badly, that after two semesters I was grateful that I had not killed them and they had not killed me." In reflecting upon the reasons for the poor communication, she said, "I think they were all upper-middle class. They had their own television sets and stereos and computers at home, as well as ten-speed bikes and all that sort of thing. All very different." Her previous students, at a state university, mostly came from farming towns, and teacher-student relations were very positive. The private college students had connections and career expectations which made them different. "They all expected to be professionals, but they didn't have a clear idea of what being a professional meant, excepting that you wore a suit, carried a briefcase, and went out to lunch every day." She continued, "Young people from families like that, of that social class, will have a nice introduction to a nice company. They will be given a shot at the bottom of the career ladder, an actual career ladder." The crux of this advantage, she concluded, is "that it really does make a difference who you know. And they all knew somebody." This comparison of students who come from privileged versus disadvantaged backgrounds, and the ease of communication with them, was a recurring theme among my respondents. Marcia's repeated allusions to the advantages of privilege and class-based networks as a precursor to employment echo her own exclusion from the employment of her choice.

Marcia's current position is, as she described it, "the lowest rung on the administrative ladder" at a prestigious university. She recalled the irony of the day when she applied for her first position at this university. When she finished her doctorate, "I used to chuckle to myself. At least I'm done with this degree. Nobody will be able to give me another test. Well, it was about nine years later, and I was sitting at [this] university, taking a typing test."

Marcia blamed gender discrimination for much of what caused the "abrupt halt" to her career aspirations.

> I wish it hadn't taken me as long as it did to realize that all the stupid jokes about women were not just jokes. I was 30 before I realized that. I thought they were just dumb jokes. It took me that long to realize that they meant them, and that they were a part of a view of the world that was going to make it very difficult for me to be taken seriously. I would not be seen in the same way as other young people starting out in my profession who happen to be men. I would just never be seen in the same way.

Marcia also believed that this awareness is still lacking today, despite evidence from life stories such as her own. She thought that she was treated equally in school up until she finished her terminal degree. "I sailed along very naively, thinking that the playing field would always be level …" The career marketplace, however, was very gender biased. To her credit, however, Marcia acknowledged the role of the larger culture in socializing men to be biased: "It's not that they are demons. It's that they have been raised to see the world in a certain way. Their vision has been protected by their own instinct for self-preservation … what they have been trained to see and what they allow themselves to see. Sometimes if that's all they see, they make major mistakes … as I think they made with me. I think I would have been an asset to their damn faculty."

In Marcia's years working in other than her chosen field, she felt disrespected by her employers because of her gender, but also disrespected because of her position. "They had absolutely no idea who I was, what I was about, what I was doing. I didn't cause them any trouble, but as for being noticed, heavens no…. I was just irrelevant." Marcia felt that being unnoticed as a full human being was equivalent to disrespect. Marcia reported that she has come to a point in her life now where she does not expect to go further, career-wise; "It's very difficult for me by now to send out the letter and the resume. So many of them have come back…. Not making the first cut, because of the Ph.D. and now because of my age…. The response has been the same as if I had not sent it at all. It's emotionally very difficult." Sadly, she remarked to her sister one time, "We're all so well educated now that we appreciate, with exquisite fineness, how little difference we make."

Penny

Penny grew up in the college town where she lives and works today. The town included two higher education institutions, a research university and a smaller private college. She recalled strained town-gown relationships in her youth, and still called herself a "townie," which is typically a pejorative term applied to local residents by college students and personnel. "I think there definitely is a very elitist view, if your parents weren't connected with [the college], if you didn't have very much money, then you were somehow less desirable." Penny was one of those unique individuals who worked her way up through the system from an entry-level clerical position to a professional position as an assistant administrator. She said, "… women today couldn't do that. I don't think today they would promote someone from within without more credentials, more academic credentials. I don't think the lack of them preclude me from doing the job."

Penny recalled that her mother always worked, because her father was an alcoholic and not consistently involved in their lives. Her father had been a mechanic; her mother first a store clerk and house cleaner, then later a clerical employee. Penny's mother eventually threw her father out, saying, "'I have to have a place the girls can bring their friends. If I can't trust you or depend on you to be sober and decent, then you can't live here.'" Penny recalled pretending that her father was dead, so that her peers wouldn't know he was an alcoholic, sometimes seen "stumbling down the street."

They moved from place to place, because of difficulty in making rent payments. As her mother was able to find more stable employment, they stayed put: "My mother said that one of the reasons why we didn't move, was because they started to come up with the idea that you needed a first and last month's rent. She said, 'I had trouble even making the rent.'"

Penny showed initiative at a young age. When her family was forced to move to a "rougher school" during her fourth-grade year in an economically depressed neighborhood, she approached the school principal and asked him if she could stay in his school in a higher socioeconomic neighborhood. He stretched the rules and allowed her to stay for another year. "So I rode my bike when I could, and then when it was too snowy, I guess I walked [across town]." At the end of that year, however, she had to go to the less desirable school. She acknowledged, "The kids, they were maybe rougher, but they were still nice people." Penny's class-based sensitivities show her appreciation for the more refined, upper-class neighborhoods and schools, but also her empathy for those like herself who were confined to limited economic and educational opportunity.

Penny was active in extracurricular activities and community activities, as well as being popular in school and doing well academically. At that time, there were no sports for girls, so she was a cheerleader. "It was the only sports minded thing you could do." While she recalled that her teachers were generally supportive, "less so in my high school years," there was a focus on negative feedback regarding behavior. As noted in the literature review, teachers may focus their efforts differentially based on social class; students from higher social class backgrounds are provided academic guidance, while students from lower social class backgrounds are addressed more often regarding their conduct. "I always remember negative comments like, 'Is that any way to act …' if you're a cheerleader [and so forth]. There was more negative than positive."

Penny attended a regional high school which included students from a variety of social class backgrounds: the blue-collar "townies" and the upper-class children of academics. She recalled being independent in high school and not asking for information about her options, like many of my respondents.

As detailed in chapter 4, Penny focused her high school studies in the vocational/secretarial track to avoid a future in manual labor. She recognized, in retrospect, the cost of not even knowing the right questions to ask. She had difficulty even finding the pathway to college, much less making informed decisions about college as her peers from more advantaged socioeconomic backgrounds seemed to know how to do.

Penny based her college decision on where her then-boyfriend was going to college. She recalled, "I was really homesick, and it was not a good experience." Because of her lack of guidance, she took pre-med biology without adequate preparation. "I was just in all the wrong things.… I didn't know it at the time, though." After seven miserable months, Penny returned home. She tried again at a local private college, but was again unsuccessful. "I don't think I'm not intelligent, but I just didn't know how to study." After a dismal college year, including taking out student loans, she quit college and resumed clerical work at the local university, and has been there ever since. In discussing the options for pursuing a degree over the past few decades, she said, "I just didn't want to keep poking myself with a stick if I didn't have to.… I was doing a good job on my job, they were good jobs, and lots of positive feedback. I had a nice life, so there wasn't the need for it."

Penny's initial nonchalance about her lack of a college degree was betrayed by further conversation which revealed that she is embarrassed by her lack of credentials and often conceals this. "Well, I do try to hide the fact that I don't have a degree from people who it would matter to." She added, "I think sometimes my boss is a little embarrassed by it too." She further noted, "… the lack of degrees is certainly a disadvantage … people are still very snobbish about that …" The elitist attitudes which university professionals held regarding credentials had not escaped her notice either: "I talk to women faculty members. They'll say things like, 'Well, she only has an Ed.D., instead of a Ph.D.,' and I think, 'Horrors! [in mock disdain] Oh, I can't imagine that!' I mean, it's not even the general Ph.D. but where you got it from … There's no end to the snobbishness about degrees …" However, she added, "That's a defense mechanism of mine."

She recalled that her mother was not at all assertive, and parent-child roles reversed on occasions which called for that. "… Even when I was 12, I would call to inquire about apartments and stuff." She explained that her mother was "… always really scared by authority. And I found out later that the reason she didn't come to school very much, like to PTA meetings, was because she never thought she had the clothes to wear." Penny related this, with anger in her voice, to the "snobbish" attitudes of the college town. Penny recalled giving her mother a pep talk for her clerical job interview: "I remember walking her up to her job interview … and I said, 'Now, I know you can do this,' because she was really scared."

One of Penny's life themes, according to her, has been "Question Authority." "I always loved that expression," she added, noting that "I have a big chip on my shoulder." Her attitude is perhaps more a valuable psychological defense against the perceived elitist atmosphere of the environment than the negative disposition suggested by the idea of having a "chip" on her shoulder.

Penny's first marriage was to a "womanizer"; after her divorce she remarried and had two daughters later in life. Her family has been central to her life, yet her early experiences have caused difficulties in her personal relationships. "I don't want to get too close to people, because I don't want them to hurt me. If I'm not too close, then they can't hurt me.… that's been a serious problem in my personal relationships. My independence." She added, "I just didn't want to be dependent on a man for anything. I never wanted to say, 'May I have $5 to go somewhere?'" She expressed difficulty in relating to her sisters, both of whom are homemakers. Now in her 50's, Penny said that she felt she had no further career options, and expected to retire from her current position.

Susan

Susan was a young woman working in admissions for a mid-sized community college. Although she grew up in a blue-collar family, she recalled that she had the advantage of being the youngest child of five, so more financial resources were available to her when it came to college choices.

Susan's father did not finish high school; he was an electrical lineman, and eventually a foreman. Her mother, who completed high school, was a homemaker and deli clerk in a grocery store. Susan grew up in a suburban area within close commuting distance of a major city. At an early age, she knew she was different from her siblings. She said she was "assertive," "outgoing," and "independent," as well as being academically talented. Her parents promoted the value of education as "the key to everything."

Although Susan was a high achiever in school, she recalled specific effects of social class on course placement in high school. Susan's remarks on having to advocate for herself to get into advanced placement courses are included in chapter 4. Her parents, though they believed in the power of education, did not have the background nor possibly the inclination to confront school authority figures on her behalf.

Susan further recalled that she felt as though she had to prove herself, both to her teachers and to her parents. "I always kind of felt that I wasn't as good as somebody. I don't know who … I almost went overboard, I had to get all A's." This level of determination to excel carried over into her college years and, later, into the workplace.

Susan, who also found guidance at the high school level seriously lacking, always wanted to "go away" to college; and recalled, "This is not a family that, you went away to college." The pressure to stay near home was great. As she said, "They knew nothing about college, never mind having me be 400 miles away." She initially chose a private college within commuting distance of home, but followed the inner call the following year by transferring to a state college farther away from home (still within the state). Although her parents were still hesitant about this choice because of the distance involved, she was able to garner their lukewarm support by demonstrating to them that the cost would be the same.

Susan's first career goal, encouraged by her parents, was to be a teacher. "They loved that because they could hold on to that, 'This is my daughter, the teacher,' ..I think that had to do with their upbringing, their background. You were to be trained to have a career, so teaching was perfect. It fit their mold." She continued, "I changed my major to psychology, and that threw them completely off. My father kept saying, 'Well what are you being trained to do exactly?'" She added, "That was a hard thing for them to grasp. They didn't get that." Her family likewise found the idea of advanced study beyond the baccalaureate confusing, although they were happy to have her living at home again while she commuted to a nearby graduate program. Her high-school friends found her continuation of study at the master's level hard to understand. "Everybody joked, 'Well, you just don't want to graduate from college.'"

Her career transitions have been difficult for her family to comprehend as well. "[My father] thought college would be the be-all, end-all of everything … I think they thought I was going to walk right into a $50,000-a-year job … like college would solve all your problems." However, Susan found a competitive job market awaiting her when she completed her M.S. in student personnel services. She recalled sending out over 100 resumes, with few interviews in her preferred career area. She finally accepted a position at a considerable distance from home, "even though it wasn't exactly what I wanted." She now has held a position which she enjoys, in the same location as her first professional position, and noted that there is a cost in terms of family: "I'm not really involved in their lives. Family problems will arise or my parents will be ill, and I'll be 500 miles away. That's hard. So I think it's more the emotional closeness to my family that it's really cost me." At the same time, she recognized the cost of her years of intensive work and study in college, and now in a competitive professional marketplace, to her social life: "It cost me a little bit more of my social life, but to me it was worth it." As in her college years, she continues to have little free time to spend with friends or in forming a long-term intimate relationship.

Susan didn't have to look far to see where her work ethic came from; like many other respondents, even if work values were not specifically discussed at home, they needed only observe their parents to see the meaning of work in their lives.

> I remember my dad being sick hardly ever … He got up, went to work early, he worked overtime. The biggest thing that was pushed [was] that you are reliable. You are dependable. You're a hard worker. Even if it was never said, through watching him, that's what was important.

Her father was not the only model for hard work; of her mother, Susan said, "I never remember her being sick, calling in sick … [She] was always on time, was furious if she ever had to be late." She added, "Through their example, that's kind of how I work." She described her work style in similar terms: arriving early, working late, working weekends. "I'm a conscientious worker," she said, "I very rarely call in sick."

I asked Susan to reflect on similarities and differences between her high-school friends, and her current friends. She noted that her current social circle includes people who have "the same work ethic" and "the same value structures", also that some have "the same kind of backgrounds" in terms of social class and upbringing. However, she described some of her old friends from a very heterogeneous school as "drifting."

> There's one friend in particular who came from a higher socioeconomic background, she graduated from Dartmouth with a degree in religion or phi-

losophy, and she's singing in a band, and working in a bar in San Francisco … I just don't know if she lived in this town, if we would really jive. I don't know if we'd really connect any more.

This disconnection from hometown friends was not uncommon among the respondents; however, it often was a disconnection from blue-collar friends whose lifestyles no longer matched the professional, middle-class lifestyles of the respondents.

Susan's career motivation was very much linked to her high school and college experiences. She recalled the lack of information, the lack of mentoring, and the lack of emotional support from people who could relate to the "bumpy road" of college, graduate school, and career transitions. The inaccurate message from her peers and from her parents was of a smooth road. "From my parents' point of view, they thought, you finish your bachelors degree in four years. You come out. You have a job. You stay in that job for the rest of your life." She noted, "Not everybody has the straight and narrow path." She reported feeling especially called to work with community college students, who are very diverse in background, age, academic preparation for college study, financial status, and need for emotional support. She has found it both "exciting" and "rewarding" in ways that she feels other higher education institutions are not. "You never really know who's going to come walking through the door, or what they are going to say … It's definitely not a cookie cutter kind of school."

Kim

Entering the college to meet Kim, I immediately noticed the difference between the mood of this small campus and the type of student, and the research university I had recently visited. This was an inner-city location, and there were two security guards stationed at the entrance, although it was mid-day. The students were primarily African-American, mostly young, and their attire had a trendy city flair. Kim was a 30-something mid-level administrator in the community college. Her particular position has focused on students who come from disadvantaged backgrounds and are currently on public assistance. They are high-risk students in the college setting.

Kim came from a rural town in which her mother was a homemaker and later worked in clerical positions, and her father worked his way up from the factory floor to a foreman position, and later owned his own business. The business went bankrupt when she was in fifth grade. As she was growing up, she recalled that finances were restricted because they lived on one income, had one car. "I remember it being really not a good car [laughs] not a reliable car, being embarrassed of that."

Unlike most of the other respondents, Kim said "school did not come very easily for me." She added, "I had a comprehension problem when I was younger .. I couldn't sit still, I was very hyper .. I really had to work a lot harder than most of the other kids." Although she encountered academic difficulties, she recalled being popular with her classmates, athletically talented, and was generally recognized as "a leader". She recalled, "I was very coordinated, very athletic; that was something my dad pushed, not the academics."

Similar to experiences revealed by a number of other respondents, Kim related, "A guidance counselor once told me that I'd never go to college, and that I'd never make it in college, I wasn't smart enough. I still, to this day, know his name, and I'd love to go back to him and say, NOW look!" She continued, "You would think a guidance counselor would be motivating kids, not de-motivating. Although it ended up motivating me."

Graduating from high school with an unremarkable record, Kim went to a nearby community college to play soccer. She said she "realized college wasn't that hard," and then "I excelled" and maintained a GPA of at least 3.0 during her community college years. When asked about her motivation and sudden academic turnaround, she said,

> It finally clicked with me that the only way to get what I wanted was through education. I don't remember that being incorporated in the K-12. Careers, talking about careers, talking about the value of education. I don't ever remember that being talked about, either with my parents or at school.

She continued, "When I got to college I saw different role models." She credited the change of environment, from a small-town high school to a more cosmopolitan city-suburban college setting, with exposing her to new experiences.

From the community college, Kim transferred to a four-year state college, majoring in psychology. She said, "I always knew I wanted to work with people." This was her first experience living away from home, and she said she did not do well. After an adjustment period, however, she was successful. She recalled that she received no encouragement to continue on for further study beyond the baccalaureate. "There weren't any mentors or anything at all." In looking back, she felt she had "a lack of knowledge about the working world."

Upon receiving the B.S. in psychology, she obtained employment as a nanny. She soon decided to try graduate school, and was admitted to a counselor education program for the M.S. In reflecting upon her choice, she has felt that she may have "jumped the gun" because of her youth, inexperience, and lack of guidance. The decision was a haphazard one: "I don't even know why I picked [state college]. I knew they had a program, I looked into it, I went for an interview and the next thing you know I was going there ... it seems like things happened so quickly."

During her undergraduate and graduate years, Kim worked full-time while enrolled as a full-time student. This was not new to her; she said, "I worked starting at the age of 13 in the factory, actually doing factory work.... I worked all through my childhood with my father." When I asked her why she was working, she responded, "My parents didn't have a lot of money to give to us. I wanted nice clothes, I wanted spending money." In addition to college work-study jobs, Kim also worked in the shopping mall, in the pizza parlor, and in a daycare center.

Kim worked at another college in a counselor position, then returned to the site of her positive associate's degree experience for employment, where she has remained for four years, including a promotion. Her parents' work values (she refers to her father as a 'workaholic') were much the same as her own. She noticed, as did other respondents, that her colleagues do not necessary share these values. She noted that some of her colleagues just come; it's just a job for them. For Kim, however, "it's never been just a job."

Kim has noticed some gender discrimination in the workplace. "I would say one of the obstacles I'm still overcoming is the fact that I'm a female.... If I'm in a meeting with my boss, who's a male, and I disagree with him, I'll get loud, my voice will elevate, and he'll say, 'OK, don't get emotional.'" She also felt that her relative youth has been a disadvantage, "my age has always been an issue."

One of the overarching themes in Kim's adult life has been the need to prove herself. "That I'm capable. That I'm intelligent. That I can do a good job. That I'm smart. I still don't see myself as smart. I see myself as motivated, not smart." She described herself as "driven," and related that this is an issue presently in her marital relationship. She was expecting their first child, and her husband would like her to decrease her work hours. She not only has worked long hours at her job and has brought work home, but worked additional hours evenings and weekends as an adjunct faculty member. She said, "I was taught that in order to get somewhere you have to work hard. You have to work very hard. You have to drive."

Kim's relationships with old high school friends were seemingly at a transition point. "I have one girlfriend who is a hairdresser and her husband works at [a university] lab. I know that they don't make as much money as we do, and that their growth for income has probably stopped, versus ours, which will probably continue to grow." In relation to these friendships, she noted that "My husband sometimes says that he feels funny talking with them about things that we're doing [like building an addition on the house and decorating it], and that he doesn't want people to feel a certain way." When pressed further on this subject, Kim shared, in a somewhat conspiratorial tone, that they had recently hired "a cleaning lady." Kim said she told her husband, "'Do not tell anybody that we have a cleaning lady,' because I'm embarrassed about that."

Kim's colleagues were surprised to learn that she was a first-generation college student from a blue-collar background. "Their image is that I had come from a middle class, educated background … They say, 'Why didn't you tell us before?', as if that would have made a difference."

The biographical sketches above provide a basis for thinking about similarities in the lived experience of women from blue-collar backgrounds who are now professionals in higher education. The nuances of individual experience, while certainly valuable, are only part of the meaning one could discern in these cases; the striking parallels across experiences are immediately apparent. Consistent with the themes identified in the focus group interview, these individuals demonstrated a similar pattern of experiences and life transitions from their earliest years in the family, through elementary and secondary education, continuing in postsecondary education, early career, and finally in their current personal and professional lives.

The primary purpose of presenting these individual biographies was not only to provide descriptive information, but also to provide an introduction to the recurring patterns and themes which will be discussed in the following chapter.

7

Life on the Margins

In my original research I identified seven major themes which cut across cases. Subsequent study and additional sharing of stories from men and women across the country have confirmed the existence of these themes in the lives of individuals from lower social class backgrounds who strive for achievement in education and careers. These themes are: gender discrimination, family as anchor, language as symbol, the new impostor syndrome, the lone(ly) ranger, the undiscussable nature of class, and members of the club. In this chapter, each theme is described in depth with supporting evidence from the interviews and additional narratives. The themes overlap in many instances, and these intersections are also noted.

Gender Discrimination

In 1979, Pierre Bourdieu noted that we can tell a great deal about social class by examining gender roles within classes. "Sexual properties are as inseparable from class properties as the yellowness of a lemon is from its acidity: a class is defined in an essential respect by the place and value it gives to the two sexes and to their socially constituted dispositions.... and the division of labour between the sexes takes quite different forms, both in practices and in representations, in the different social classes."[90] Gender discrimination is not news. However, it was so pervasive in the life stories of the women I interviewed that to ignore it would be remiss. Discrimination against women was the backdrop against which their personal and professional lives were enacted. Based on the perceptions of the research participants in my original study, it was clear that gender discrimination took place in a myriad of social relationships and social settings: in the family of origin, in the schools, in colleges and universities, in marital relationships, and in the workplace. In short, it so permeated the lifespan, as these interviewees described it, that it seems fair to conclude that gender discrimination is embedded in American culture.

The discrimination described here was often obvious and unmistakable, but just as frequently subtle and covert. Sharon suggested that as a young student (about 20 years ago), she didn't notice it; she said that currently, "I think my students here at [university] don't really notice[91]". She continued, "I think really it's only when you get older that you notice it, and you start getting really pissed off [laughs]."

Additional forms of discrimination were part of the experience of several interviewees, on the basis of age (either being too young or too old in the occupational marketplace), race/ethnicity, or career field. Although it is not within the purview of this book to address these additional forms of discrimination, it must be noted that these discriminatory practices intersect with gender and take on an added intensity. Are male employers equally intimidated by young men who have good credentials, as they were by Jennifer, whom they refused to hire because she was young and "overqualified"? Or would they be delighted to hire someone (male) so highly qualified?

Examples of gender discrimination in the family have been cited previously in this book, both in the description of the focus group interview, and in the individual cases. You will recall Karen saying that her father was very sexist, and that the family resources were channeled to her brothers. Eileen's mother discouraged Eileen's higher education aspirations in much the same way: the boys in the family would have to support a family one day, after all. Sharon's father warned her against taking jobs away from men, and Stephanie's father (he of the many mistresses) wondered why she was sitting down eating rather than serving her husband dinner. Linda's father promoted a message of value for education to her brothers; she said, "They had no idea that I was listening".

In the elementary and secondary school years, gender differences in treatment were apparent. Jennifer, whose school days were more recent than many in the group, recalled a specific lack of encouragement for female students. She credited her notice of this social fact with her exposure to one female English teacher who had them read some "feminist" writers: Gloria Steinem and Betty Friedan. Marcia recalled being a bit uncomfortable in her high school physics class: "When I found myself the only girl in the class, I wasn't as uncomfortable as I might have been, if I had realized the full implications." The underlying message was that girls weren't supposed to be in science classes. Pat recalled that it was OK for her to be smart in high school, because in doing so she was not a threat to the males, who focused on sports. Penny recalled participating in cheerleading because at that time, "it was the only sports minded thing girls could do." According to the stories of younger respondents, sports teams are no longer strictly male territory;

but their experience is that gender imbalance remains in school expenditures for male versus female sports, as well as participation rates.

Elsewhere in this book, I note that not only family but also school personnel steered the respondents towards traditional female roles: wife, mother, secretary, nurse, and teacher. The few women who had attended Catholic secondary schools recalled the nuns who served as teachers as "strong, admirable and well-educated women" who served as positive role models for them. However, the existence of such models who had limited their own career pursuit according to religious doctrine and practice did not provide a completely effective counterbalance to the gender-biased messages the respondents were otherwise receiving.

In undergraduate school, Sharon recalled male faculty members who "said that women couldn't be as good public citizens as men, and women were not as qualified as men." She argued with them. She also recalled that she had only studied with one female faculty member during all of her undergraduate years.

Karen's situation perhaps best exemplified the mixed messages which these women received from their families regarding educational achievement. Her father's sister was the only person on either side of the family who had gone to college, and was a school teacher during Karen's youth. This person "was an important figure in the family" and was pointed to as someone to emulate. She encouraged Karen, but only up to a point. When Karen did go to college and beyond, the relationship was over: "… she started being very threatened by me, that I would go to college and go to graduate school, so she disappeared out of my life."

Pat recalled her years as a graduate student and how the imbalance of gender affected her: "I was frightened or fearful all of the time. I was one female student out of a class of 15 guys. I taught solely with guys. The instructors I worked with before were all men."—and this was not in a traditionally male field. Sharon concurred, noting that "there are certain kinds of obstacles and unpleasantries that one encounters in graduate school. Especially if one is a woman." Karen noticed subtle discrimination in graduate school, but she questioned her interpretation of it: "you can't tell how much of the things that happened to you really had to do with being a woman in a field that wasn't a women's field."

In the workplace, gender discrimination has been evident in employment practices such as who gets hired, in what position, and for what pay. Jennifer noted that although there are women administrators at her institution, she could also see the "glass ceiling." This has also been called the "leaky pipeline," as discussed in greater detail previously.

Jennifer was also aware of being paid less than what she should have received based on pay equity guidelines. She might have filed an employment grievance, but given her difficulty in securing employment, she did not wish to jeopardize her employment standing by doing so.

Because of gender discrimination in employment, many of the respondents mentioned having no female role models or mentors either in college as students, or later as employees themselves. Pat said, "There weren't many [women] in those years. You would find your one woman per department, unless it was English." When there were women in such positions, they appeared to be very visible against an otherwise all-male backdrop. During her graduate school years, Jennifer recalled first considering a career in higher education because of a female role model: "I was influenced a lot by women in higher education, seeing what they did, and thinking, I like this. I could do this too." This was especially important for Jennifer, whose primary role model at home presented quite a different picture. Her mother clearly hated her job and "couldn't wait to retire.... I knew I didn't want that. I didn't want to work in a place where I couldn't stand it." At the same time, however, Jennifer's mother modeled hard work and independence at home, as opposed to Jennifer's stepfather, who she said "has never, never done much around the house or helped her out at all. She maintained a full-time job, raised three kids, and did everything there was to do."

Stephanie also noted the importance of a female role model in her graduate school years. She said, "It was the first-hand knowledge of and exposure to my mentor ... realizing that, this was a [viable] occupational choice ..." Only one respondent did not mention any female role models during her school years; however, Kim spoke of a mentor in her current employment situation, a female administrator who "sends me articles, and meets with me every so often." This person was also encouraging Kim's career aspirations and the possibility of her continuing her education at the doctoral level.

Pat brought up the point that gender discrimination was sometimes applied to entire departments. By way of example, she told of a downsizing period during the early years of her career when selected departments (other than her own) were eliminated, "They just axed everybody in women's studies." In other words, those departments most populated by women were the most vulnerable to cuts. Karen expanded upon this point, saying, "There's an advantage to being in a place that has more women, but the disadvantage is that it automatically doesn't get very much respect." Because of the political nature of higher education environments, she concluded, "It doesn't help to have a lot of women. That also causes problems." The problems to which she refers seem to include disrespect and a higher probability of job loss based on the fact of femaleness.

Because of continuing discrimination in higher education employment practices, Pat noted that "I don't have a lot of female colleagueship. I have to go to the English department to talk to women faculty." As a new faculty member in her late 20's, Stephanie also found that her new department "doesn't have very many female faculty." She felt that she was in competition with the male faculty members, and said, "I want to prove that I can be as good as them ... that a female can do it." There seemed to be some underlying assumption in higher education, as a workplace, that women do not do as good a job, are not as competent.

Pat also felt that her male colleagues had difficulty relating to her. "I think that it was because I was a working woman, as opposed to a suburban non-working woman, or a professional's wife." She added, "So I think there is a layer of class there as well." Sharon noted that she felt "alienated from male administrators" but was uncertain whether that was a function of gender or class. Karen also voiced confusion over gender- versus class-based discrimination: "You never know the source of this sense that there's a world going on out there that you just can only partly, barely see. Sometimes it does have to do with being a woman. Sometimes it has to do with where you come from."

Karen shared some information on a period in her career when she worked in a department where half of the faculty were women. "That changes the whole dynamic of the [department]. Sometimes we forget how much, but it really does." When asked to expand upon the difference, she recalled a colleague saying of her current employment, "This is sort of a cutthroat place because you've got all these men." Karen was relatively comfortable, however, because her undergraduate and graduate education had prepared her for this imbalance: "I had come from an environment that was mostly men, so I know what that was like." Marcia described a similar situation in her current department, but used a different label: "There is a very, very strong corporate culture here. It is male." She went on to say that the culture is based on constant competition, the goal of which is to establish and re-establish hierarchical relationships. The competition is conducted in what Marcia saw as a particularly vicious manner, including verbal warfare and duplicitous behavior. "It's not pleasant to watch," Marcia concluded.

In marriage relationships, women have typically been in more vulnerable roles, financially and physically if not otherwise. In response to a question about whether she had ever felt not respected, Sharon replied, "Only when I was married and being abused." Rita recalled her mother encouraging education as a safety net: "If marriage doesn't go well you don't have to tolerate it. It [education] empowers a woman." She recalled later in our conversation that her mother socialized her to cook, clean, and basically play a domestic role: "The message is, I wasn't supposed to be a professional. It happened by accident." As a single woman, Rita also understood the social context from whence this message came. In talking about women from her generation (she is in her 40's), she said, "if you were single, it really pulled you down quite a bit economically." Therefore, marriage was encouraged for the purpose of financial security. Similarly, Marcia recalled that her father opposed the idea of her and her sister going to college, "on the grounds that we ought not be too well educated. It would hurt our chances at marriage." In a related vein, Marcia, who remained single, noted that she felt discriminated against as a single woman. She said, "The great myth that they keep trying to sell you in the newspapers is that women must choose between careers and family." Since she was unmarried, she has been perceived by others as having actively chosen career and rejected marriage; although this was not the case.

The overlap of the variables of gender and social class appeared repeatedly in the narratives of the interviewees, and this overlap was apparent to them. As Sharon put it, "I think there's certain kinds of disadvantages that come from being born female. Not as many doors are open to you." She continued, "I can't tell whether it's being a woman or having been born in a different class." Rita echoed this, saying that it is a struggle for women in higher education careers, "especially women from working-class backgrounds." Although it is difficult to separate gender effects from class effects, it seems certain that the combination of gender and social class has an intensifying effect in their experiences.

In conclusion, the crux of the matter appears that these women from working-class backgrounds learned first what they—as females—could not do or should not do as females in America; what was inappropriate for them to aspire to. There were too few female role models and mentors, but luckily the appearance of these increased as they progressed to higher and higher levels of education. The interviewees were socialized to their appropriate roles, then left to figure out for themselves what remained for them to do. The emphasis was not on opportunities, but on limits. Much of these limits were based on gendered conceptions of what is possible and appropriate for women in American culture. Added intensity came from what was conceivable and, questionably, advisable for females from the lower social classes.

Family as Anchor

The pull of family appeared over and over again in the stories of the interviewees. The terms "pull" and "anchor" purposely leave the question of directionality open, and the meaning indefinite. Family could provide a secure base from which to explore education and career opportunities, or family could convey a sense of being pulled down or held back from achieving. Both of these possible meanings were illustrated in conversation with the interviewees, often at the same time. The family which served as a secure base could also be the family which held one back.

The family of origin exerted a strong influence on these women's college choices, sometimes encouraging college aspirations, sometimes constructing geographic boundaries beyond which they were not to venture, sometimes providing clearly limited support for higher aspirations than those delineated by the family. The respondents' relationships with significant others (spouses and partners) continued in the same vein, with limitations based on relationship concerns and gender role constraints. At the same time, as mothers today many of the respondents with children noted that their choices were constrained by family concerns such as safety for their children in an increasingly violent society, and questions regarding the values their children were learning. A cycle of disconnection with the family of origin—parents and siblings—and uncertain reconnection in adulthood seemed to serve dual purposes: emotional recovery for the respondent, and fulfilling a caretaking role for aging parents. The respondents also took upon themselves the task of acting as role models and mentors for working-class nieces and nephews, encouraging their higher aspirations. Beyond mere gender role socialization typical of American culture, the interviewees' working-class roots played a part in intensifying the message of traditional roles for females, and in the development and implementation of educational and career choices.

Many families made it difficult for their daughter to leave home to attend college. In several cases, like those of Rita, Charlene, and Nancy, they were the only one in their family to go to college. Lack of prior experience with this transitional moment was a problem in itself. Although at least one parent of most interviewees supported their daughter's educational aspirations (with limits), they wanted her to stay at (or very near) home. Those who left, like Pat, recalled guilt feelings: "I felt like I was deserting my father and my brother." In contrast, Sharon's family made life so difficult for her that she needed to leave home. She recalled of those years, "I liked school. It was my family I didn't like." Thus, she was quite happy to leave, and her parents' opposition had little impact on her decision. Disconnection with the family was, for her, a positive event.

Karen wanted to get away from her rural environment because, "There were no jobs for me there ... there was nothing for me to do, and I just wanted to go somewhere far away." Her father opposed her leaving, but she was able to leave the state in a compromise selection: "[State U.] was far enough away for me, and close enough for him ... it was a day's drive away, so it was OK. So I went there." The reader will recall that Karen's choice of a major field of study was in an attempt to please her father, and to gain his attention and approval, again attesting to the pull of family.

Susan had difficulty breaking away from her family; as the youngest, it was especially hard to leave "because nobody ever went away to college." Part of the problem was that her parents "knew nothing about college." Although Kim's parents were neutral about the idea of college, she acknowledged that, "they don't know what it's all about, and I think it was probably scary for them."

Stephanie's mother had always encouraged her to pursue a college education; however, her father "did not care one bit about education." According to Stephanie, her father "really didn't understand." For Stephanie, whose mother had been supportive throughout high school but who fell apart in the aftermath of her divorce from Stephanie's father, leaving home for college was not a viable option. Stephanie needed to work and help her younger sisters through their youth while her mother recovered. She said, "It wasn't really an option for me to go away to school, because I was kind of the main figure in the family." She attempted to gain emotional distance from her family by moving on campus. She recalled, "I felt that it was 'me' time. You know, time for Stephanie to have a life." A crisis occurred at home, however, which involved all family members, the police, and an ambulance. She related her resulting feelings of guilt for having left home: "At that point I realized that, what I did was probably wrong." She moved back home and curtailed her extracurricular activities; her life revolved around academics, family, work, and her boyfriend.

The draw of significant relationships was not restricted to families of origin. Several women, like Jennifer and Penny, reported making college choices based on where their boyfriend was going to college. Regardless of her boyfriend's presence, Penny recalled having a bad case of homesickness (even though she had not left the state). Other respondents recalled the emotional toll that leaving home had taken as well.

The disconnection with family which began with undergraduate leave-taking was, for many, just the beginning of an uncomfortable process of separation. Pat recalled inviting her father, sister, and brother to her doctoral graduation ceremony. Although she felt they were proud of her, she regretted the choice. Seeing them in her environment, she realized just how huge the gap was between her life and their lives. "I guess I hadn't anticipated them seeming so out of place. And I think they were not only out of place, but resented even having to be there. So I had to tap more into the reality of, this is not their world, never will be their world. I need to wake up and let it go. Let them go their way. Let me have mine."

Like Pat, Jennifer presented a similar instance of inconsistent emotional messages from family members from pride to resentment. Jennifer's parents were neutral about her college aspirations; she recalled that "there wasn't a lot of encouragement." Although she thought that they "probably felt good that I went to college," there were repercussions later. Her mother's resentment appeared as Jennifer's educational achievement soared: "After I got my master's degree, my mother made comments like, what do I think, do I think I'm better than them, or better than her or something? ... of course they all said they're proud of me." She continued on to explain that her stepfather was bitter when she landed her first professional job: "When he found out the salary I was making, he said, 'I've worked here 25 years and I'm only making five or six thousand dollars more than that.'" Instead of pride, Jennifer encountered resentment from her parents. She concluded, "We're not really a family any more ... not close at all by any means."

Educational and professional achievement, combined with social class background and gender rules, appear to have had effects regarding the respondents' marital relationships. Marriage for some respondents came early; perhaps too early. Pat said that she dropped out of college to get married in part to "try to have some independence from my father". The marriage did not last; she recalled of her ex-husband, "He wanted to be married and not married at the same time, like most 20-year-old guys." Divorce was not uncommon in this group. Values were sometimes at least part of the reason for marriages breaking up. Sharon recalled that her ex-husband, who came from a higher social class background, "did not have the sense that people had worth regardless of education, and people had worth regardless of what sort of work they did." In contrast, she felt strongly that people are of equal worth, regardless of degree or occupational status. She wryly noted that until her marriage, she had assumed that all people shared her views on this.

Stephanie also dropped out of college and married young. When the marriage became seriously troubled, she tried to return home; however, her mother sent her back to her husband, saying "You're married now. You're a big girl. You've got to take responsibility for your relationship. You need to go back to your husband and work this out." When she did get divorced, however, Stephanie's mother welcomed her back home, a home which was now a safe haven.

Karen did not drop out of college to get married; she was able to stay in college after her marriage to a fellow student who came from a similar background. Like many women of her generation, she worked not only to support herself, but to keep her husband in school, since he needed her financial support. When her marriage ended many years later, this was the catalyst for a period of reflection, transition and growth. She recalled it as "a watershed moment." This was a pattern among other respondents as well, who re-evaluated career goals, personal values, and individual attributes in the wake of divorce.

Sharon wondered whether her career success had exacted a cost in terms of her marriage. One of the points of friction had been that she wished to remain in her position as a tenured faculty member at a top-tier research university; he expected her to follow him to a less well-respected institution for the sake of his career. He left; she stayed.

When Penny's first husband decided to move away, she quit her job to follow him; she recalls being rather miffed when he changed his mind after it was too late for her to rescind her resignation. Several years later, Penny recalled with obvious enjoyment how supportive her family was when she left her womanizing husband. She said, "My older sister was surprisingly assertive about it. I didn't find out some of the things that she did behind my back [until later], like calling my husband at work and saying, 'Don't you show up at her apartment again, or you're going to regret it.'"

A number of women reported strained marital relationships because of their assertiveness and fierce independence. Echoing Penny's words, noted previously, Stephanie said, "I was never going to ever put myself in a position where I had to rely on a man, or rely upon anyone, to make it." She added that her husband said that "he found it hard to really get in that last wall" in forming an intimate relationship with her because of these personal characteristics.

Rita has found that her mother's prediction was accurate: "You can't get married and go to school [both]." Her love relationship was not able to survive doctoral studies. A single woman in academe, she said that long-term relationships are incompatible with the overwhelming demands of the profession: "You end up with a man who is going to be demanding" and there isn't time or energy for the two of them. "So it's a double whammy," she concluded. Without family nearby, without a spouse/partner or children, she said, "I'm like a plant without roots."

Marcia also never married; she noted with clarity that unmarried women in America are not considered normal. She said, "It has been [very] significant in my life that I never married. It's a lot easier for a woman to be seen, as she is seen, as half of that social unit. It makes it easier for the people who make the decisions, to place you." When asked to expand upon what that meant, she replied, "Just place you in their understanding of the universe." Marcia seemed to feel that she had been excluded from certain job opportunities because she did not fit the "normal" mold of an adult female in our society; i.e., she should be married or something is wrong with her.

Family disconnections were never complete and rarely permanent. Ironically, although Pat left home to go to college, her father, sister, and brother ended up following her to another state and city, and settled near her. "They all live in my town now. All of them." Although she had career opportunities out of the area, she said, "I felt compelled to stay ... I still felt a commitment to family to stay there ... So I stayed, but I was sort of aching to leave."

Stephanie found it extremely difficult to leave her family of origin to accept a very attractive job offer at a considerable distance. "It was very hard for me to choose to come [here] .. all my family is down there. And being the first daughter, and to all of a sudden say, now I'm going to leave .." She reported that it was the most difficult decision she had yet made. Susan had a similar experience. She noted that all of her siblings live near her parents, and so it was extremely difficult for her to take a job at a considerable distance from home. "In order to get the job that I really wanted to get, I had to move away." She thought that if she had not moved for her career, however, "I don't know if I would have been as successful, if I hadn't gotten independent." At the same time, it was clear from her remarks that the emotional cost to moving away from family could not be ignored. In other cases, like that of Rita, it seemed that a tenure-track faculty career required one to put family second, no matter how unnatural that may have felt.

Some women's families were instrumental in aiding their daughters in pursuing career opportunities, some were neutral, and some were simply unwilling to help. Jennifer recalled that her parents fell into the latter group; they were unwilling to help her out of a disastrous relationship and long-term unemployment crisis in a distant state. Jennifer recalled being "desperate" for help at the time. She had been closer with her grandparents since her childhood, and fortunately, her grandmother was there for her financially and emotionally, even though she was living on social security. Jennifer's bitterness at her parents' perceived abandonment of her was still evident.

As established higher education professionals, the women typically reported that their parents were proud of their achievement. Stephanie reported of her mother, "She's incredibly proud of me." Sharon, who managed to reconnect with her parents (at the urging of her sister) after decades of estrangement, said, "Now my mother's so happy [laughs] that I'm this college professor, after she was a homemaker." However, like the family's lack of understanding of advanced degree study which Rita related, there were gaps in family relationships based on gaps in understanding of higher education careers. Sharon said, "There are always aspects of my work that my family don't really understand. There's certain kinds of things that I tend to avoid talking about with them … It would be tough to explain to them."

Susan noted of her career choice and her parents' views on it, "They didn't get that." It was not anything they had prior exposure to, and thus could not relate to it. Similarly, Karen reported that her parents "never had even a clue about what I do. They never had anything in their lives to give them any insight into what it means to even go to college, let alone be a college professor … So I can't really talk to them about any of that." This reinforced a sense of isolation from family.

Parenting is a role most women are socialized to expect and pursue. This may be underscored in the case of blue-collar families. Pat recalled strong messages from her siblings, who married and started families in their twenties, to settle down and have a family. They let Pat know that "I should get on with it and be a parent, because what life is about is being a parent." After trying for many years to get pregnant, at the time of our interview Pat was the single mother of a young son. She noted, "Something always keeps me at home." She made many of her career choices in the past decade based on her role as a mother, and had clearly made that a priority in her life. She left a particularly demanding job because, "There wasn't enough [of me] for that and a small child." She had also decided to abandon her preferred career choice because it required her to frequently work evenings and weekends, "things that take you away from interacting with your family."

Stephanie remembered selecting higher education as a career field because she perceived it as one which would allow for a balance between work and the children she hoped to have: "I could have a lifestyle that I could have a family.… that I could be there for my kids when they got back from school." Now that she had a husband, toddler, and a faculty career, however, she was not so sure about the balance; at the time of our interview she was experiencing more of the stress of having both things. She also noted that she had seriously considered staying at home as a full-time mother, instead of accepting her current enviable position. "… over my life I had a little bit of resentment that I didn't have a mom who was at home, and now that I had a child, didn't want to have that same scenario …"

However, after long consideration and discussion with her spouse, they concurred that the job offer "could be one of those once-in-a-lifetime" opportunities. She reserved the option to re-decide on full-time motherhood at a later date if she had more children. Her child was clearly a priority; she said, "Then I have my son. I come home … I see his face and I hold him, and I realize what's really important here." As noted previously, Kim, who was about to become a mother, planned to cut back on work hours in order to bring more balance to her life and the demands that motherhood would bring.

In adulthood, many of the women I interviewed reported not being emotionally close with their siblings. Although some of that has to do with geographic separation, at least part of that psychological distance had to do with dissimilar careers. Sharon noted that her six siblings were all employed in the automotive industry. She reported that she was only close with one sister, who was dissatisfied with her current work and matched Sharon in intellectual curiosity and feminist interests. Penny was still relatively close with her sisters, but she noted some difficulty comprehending their lifestyle choices: "Both of my sisters have been homemakers, and that just blows my mind that they would do that." Echoing the earlier sentiment expressed by other respondents, she said, "I just didn't want to be dependent on a man for money."

Jennifer, as yet unmarried and childless, reported being concerned about her nephew; her sister had not attended college and worked at an entry-level job in the post office. Jennifer said that she wished someone would speak with her sister and encourage her to go back to school and better her life because "you've got a son to think of now." Similarly, Karen told of an incident in which her father recently criticized her sister's career at the cost—in his eyes—of her parenting: "She went to visit my dad recently, and he lectured her on how she ought to be staying home with her kids …" Other women without children voiced concerns regarding the children who are closest to them. Rita noted that although her siblings are in blue-collar jobs, she has been a role model for her nieces and nephews, who had looked at her educational and career success and said, "You did this, so why couldn't we?" Likewise, Susan said that she was a role model for her nieces and nephews in terms of applying to and selecting colleges. "I'm kind of mentoring them," she said.

Sharon thought about the differences in lifestyle between herself at her age, and her parents at that age. Her comments focused on changes in the social world which have had an impact on children and thus her role as a mother. In her childhood, the "society wasn't generally as violent, wasn't as unsafe. I mean, I worry about … I would never leave my kid anyplace. I always know where he is, where he's going." In her childhood, it was not unusual for children to roam around the neighborhood playing during the day, thus giving her parents "freedoms and flexibility" that she does not have as a parent today.

Penny's reflections as a married parent of two teenage daughters today were similar in tone. She recalled of her childhood, "there weren't the same kinds of dangers that there are now. I mean, even though the neighborhood was poor, it wasn't drug infested or anything like that, that you would face today." This recollection was prompted by another memory in which a mother from a higher social class had told her daughter not to play with kids like Penny, who were from the poorer side of town. "Her parents said they didn't want [her] to associate with me because of where I lived." Penny now says, "Now that I am a parent myself though, I see ... I can understand better what they were saying." Penny's perception was that those wealthier families saw poor children like herself as potentially dangerous and her lower-class neighborhood unsafe. Their warnings and prescriptions were perhaps their way of keeping their children safe from harm.

Although Penny wanted her daughters to be treated well by others, and had done her best to give them the things she could not afford to have in her youth, she expressed conflicting feelings because she wanted them to have working-class values. "I don't want them to be snobs. That would be the last thing I would want them to be." She added, "It's important to work hard and not to look down on people because they have less than you, because you don't know what their circumstances are." She found that there was a delicate balance in this matter, the boundaries of which were difficult to define with any accuracy.

Karen reported that her decision to end her marriage to an abuser had primarily focused on the welfare of her children: "My husband was actually abusive to me, and ultimately I left him because of the way he treated my kids. He didn't abuse them, but it became clear that his behavior towards me was really very important in their lives ..." She also voiced an awareness about the larger culture of higher education which devalues concerns regarding family welfare issues, which are typically women's issues. This was echoed by Rita, who felt that her institution was unjustly harsh in judging her work during the period of time around her father's death, when she was not only emotionally vulnerable, but called to perform extended family duties in the mourning period expected by her ethnic group.

Sharon, like other respondents who were mothers of young children, reported that her current choices of friends are typically other mothers of same-age children. Likewise, Stephanie was drawn to parents of young children; she felt that their family roles made them "more down-to-earth" and thus more like her, less like the "snooty" attitude commonly found in her prestigious work environment. Penny noted that her current friends are people who like "doing things with their kids."

As a mother, Pat was concerned about the values that her child was learning, growing up in the environment that surrounds higher education. She said:

> It puts me in a predicament in terms of my child, because I don't think I'm passing on the working class to him. You know, where he hangs out, is with other college people. He's only been around educated adults. He's never been around working class culture. So I'm a little disturbed in terms of what I'm creating, and will it be foreign to me … Will he be somebody that I don't even recognize or want to be around in terms of his values?

Karen shared this concern with the dissimilarity of experience that her children have: "This isn't quite the right environment. I think about my sons who have grown up in this environment, who have a really different sort of experience and understanding of what it means, than I ever will have." She added, "In some ways they have a lot more choices … they could do things differently than I ever could."

Pat further recalled an angry encounter with her sister over the topic of family and career. "I think the resentment from my sister is that I want to have my cake and eat it too. I want to have a child, and a family, and be a mother. And I want a career and an identity. And I refuse to let go of those for anyone."

In conclusion, family has the ambiguous role and power of an anchor; sometimes loving and empowering enough to act as a secure base from which to operate, sometimes dragging its daughters/wives/lovers/mothers downward, holding them back from optimal achievement. Pat said, "I don't really, maybe even today, [with] those working class roots, really feel like I had the freedom to leave family. I don't really think I ever have."

Language as Symbol

As a symbol system, language allows us to communicate in ways which are agreed upon and sanctioned by the larger culture. However, it is not just a symbol system; language itself is a symbol. How we use language is a marker of our social class background, and we are judged—and judge others—accordingly.

The topic of language and its larger meaning in the lives of women from blue-collar backgrounds appeared in the focus group interview, and subsequently in all of the individual interviews.

Early childhood recollections of the power of language in our society included Eileen's memory of "my father's inability to read." Both Eileen and Charlene admitted to some feelings of inferiority in terms of their vocabulary; even though both women reported continued efforts to increase their vocabulary, Eileen said she felt that she "never had that base" of expanded vocabulary use in the home to build upon. Charlene said, "We used to laugh about words that had more than two syllables in them. It wasn't part of the language you used with your family." Stephanie said, "I can use a lot of big vocabulary words, but I'm not comfortable with it. It's something you read in books. It's something you see in dictionaries … most of the time when you talk to me, I don't strike you as brilliant."

Charlene recalled the time when her dissertation advisor took her and her father out to lunch after the dissertation defense, and noted her father's lack of comprehension of her advisor's vocabulary: "I could see from the look on my father's face that he had no clue what [my advisor] meant. I mean, this was not a word in my father's vocabulary."

Kim saw her limited use of vocabulary as a career asset in her community college environment and in her particular position working with students from disadvantaged backgrounds. She said, "I get down on their level … I don't use big words. I can relate to them. So when students talk to me, they can tell … that I come from a certain place because of the way I talk to them." This enabled her to have a relationship with the students that was more comfortable for them, as well as for her. She said, "I don't ever place myself above [them] because I wouldn't want that. I wouldn't want to be treated that way …" She maintained a demeanor which exuded equality, and thus was careful to use language in a way which would not be construed as condescending.

Both Charlene and Penny noted that they still used profanity in their everyday language, and they saw this as a sign of their social class background. Penny noted that in her prestigious institution, appropriate language is a requirement: "I swear a lot, and I certainly can't do that at work." She adds, "It's a class thing … I don't think proper women swear …"

The limits on language as a current barrier to family communication was a repeated theme. Charlene recalled: "So where I have a language difference is when I go home. I know that there are things that I cannot say with my family because they will not understand it. There are certain words I cannot use because they will not understand it." Nancy agreed with this assessment, as it appeared in her family relationships as well. Karen recalled, "I haven't been back [home] to visit my family in a long time. When I did go back, it would be clear that I had a different way of talking, and a different set of things to talk about … So I don't belong there anymore ..." The theme of not belonging is discussed in greater depth later in this chapter.

There were differences in language content, including vocabulary and topic as described above, but there were also differences in form and purpose, as well as racial/ethnic dimensions to language style. Stephanie reported that after attending an all-black junior high school in a poorer neighborhood, and then being bused to an upper-class white school, "I had language or speech, ways of saying things or doing things, that I thought was normal, until I started hanging around white kids more. I said, 'Oh, they don't understand me.'" She modified her speech patterns to more closely resemble theirs while she was in that environment. Rita also noted that her Hispanic accent betrayed her background, and the fact that "I always mispronounce a couple of words." She said that she sees this as a combination of social class and cultural background. Susan saw her New York City accent as a sign of her social class background. She said, "My perception is that people think people with New York accents are ignorant, or they don't sound as well versed." Interestingly, she acknowledged that her accent was virtually indiscernible, but she had no conscious awareness of moderating it or having tried to disguise it.

Pam noted that for many years her use of language reflected her attempt to match prevailing norms in higher education. Now that she has become more comfortable in her career, she talked about the increasing similarity in her vocabulary and communication style at home and at work. "It's more and more the same for me, but I think there was a time when it was a real focus for me. That 'fitting in' thing." Similarly, as mentioned previously, Charlene judged her family's language use negatively, and then turned that criticism back on herself for betraying her home speech community.

The idea of a working-class "dialect" was something that appeared repeatedly. For example, Sharon, a tenured faculty member, noted that "A very colloquial style of speech comes out in my teaching, and is there is my writing too." She and Penny mentioned feeling very uncomfortable with their public speaking skills, and related this to social class background. Sharon said, "I've always felt that that inability to speak elegantly on my feet is an indicator of my class background."

Pam talked about the transition she has to make from her worksite and the type of language she uses there, to her present homelife and the type of language she uses to communicate with her partner, who comes from a background similar to her own:

So I go to work, try to do the educated thing, with the vocabulary and whatever. My partner comes from a poor background, very poor. And so there even is that class issue there. Making the transition in the five-minute ride from work to home ... I think it's about being understood on both sides. I know there's a way that I talk with people who are not at work to be understood by them, and there's a way that I talk to people at work to be understood by them. And it just seems sometimes like never the twain shall meet.

Pam said she feels the necessity to make a "superman transition" in the car as she moves from one social class environment to another, in terms of language and styles of interpersonal communication and interaction.

The purpose of language in blue-collar families can be qualitatively different from that in upper-class families. As detailed in a previous chapter, communication in blue-collar families is typically in one direction, from parent to child, and focuses on concrete and practical matters. Linda recalled infrequent communication with her father, who worked 12 or more hours a day. "Communication with him was about work ... we didn't talk big sentences, he was too busy." Similarly, Karen recalled a lack of exposure to conversation at home and the types of communication she encountered in college and beyond. As noted in chapter 4, Karen talked about her father's restricted use of language. He did not discuss any inner thoughts or feelings; rather, he used language in limited ways to direct activity or identify external things to be addressed.

An interesting characteristic of communication which each woman felt was her own eccentricity, but was in fact widely shared, was a sense of tactlessness in communication with others. Pat said, "I just blurt things out and get in trouble, and offend people, and say the wrong thing in the wrong place at the wrong restaurant." She added that this was problematic in higher education organizations where diplomacy is highly valued. Sharon also admitted to this "flaw;" but even though it seemed to her to be a "hindrance," she also saw its value: "I know that my brashness, and my bluntness, and my colloquialisms are also a rhetorical tool for me. I'm willing to get up and tell some male administrator that I think that some colleague they're trying to make me hire is a dimwit. And I think that a lot of other people might not do that." Thus, she saw a "political benefit" to this directness, if not immediately to herself, then at least to the larger institution.

Sharon viewed the "male administrators" as smooth-talking. Like other respondents, she had a perception of such glibness as dishonest. "I don't feel like I'm somebody who could lie. And I think there's a lot of deceit going on among the administration ... I feel like a lot of those male administrators feel perfectly comfortable with doing that kind of thing. In effect, lying through their teeth." Marcia held similar views on the potential of language to be duplicitous. In her current employment environment, the importance of a certain style of language for higher education administrators has been clear. She said, "The way you are supposed to talk [is important]. You have got to talk the talk ... And it is the talk that I cannot talk." She explained further, "I cannot speak in professional-ese ... There is a vocabulary, you know ... They [the administrators] are out there talking that language to each other, and there's no question in my mind that if you can learn how to manipulate it, then you can impress people ..." She said that she is "incapable" of that style of talk, and called herself "linguistically disadvantaged," although that was hardly the case in any fashion other than metaphorically speaking.

Similarly, Penny saw language as one of the obstacles to advancement in her career: "I don't talk the talk." In these cases, "talking the talk" had less to do with vocabulary and more to do with using language as a weapon, something to inflict harm upon others, preferably without them knowing it until the damage has been done and the perpetrator's role in it has been obscured.

Language can be used as a weapon, but also as a sign of exclusivity. Marcia brought up the important point that academic specialties, and administrative areas as well, have formed languages of exclusion; that is, they have a vocabulary which only they understand, and which prevents the participation of lay persons. That exclusivity, Marcia said, "is one of the major purposes for all of the professional jargons." While she believed that it originally had an honorable purpose of ease of communication among professional colleagues, it has become "a way of bonding and of communicating and of excluding and of impressing." She went on to describe a situation in her current field, like others, where the term "downsizing" has been used to describe what might be more accurately and simply referred to as firing people. Thus a smoke screen has been used to disguise the "plain honest truth." This manipulation of language in order to relieve the burden of responsibility which the institution might otherwise carry, she said, "is bad business for people's souls." Those who suffer most from such obfuscation are, ultimately, "the people whose lives their decisions will affect."

This manipulation of language for public relation purposes was elucidated further by Marcia, who said, "I think that the social contract in this country is being destroyed all around us by those who misuse language." She saw the political dimensions of the use of language, and the implications of such usage. For example, she cited politicians' and academic administrators' focus on image and packaging rather than substance; she viewed this as "patent dishonesty."

Language was discussed also in terms of silencing. Penny recalled a situation on her campus where women were sometimes faced with the unethical actions of others, and were vulnerable and thus passive: "They see something that is going wrong, but they can't say anything for fear of retaliation, or that they would be fired ..." Faced with these ethical decisions, she said, "Women, unfortunately, have to make those choices all the time."

It was not surprising, given the value of language and the hierarchical classification of language styles which devalues lower-class dialects and directness, that publication has been problematic for the women faculty I interviewed. Publication is the currency of academe, and without a considerable record of publications in top-tier journals, tenure-track faculty generally do not get tenure. This highly specialized and constrained form of language usage, which requires a style of writing and communication foreign to blue-collar families, carries a larger meaning. While it exacts a toll on the writer in its power of rejection and loaded relation to continued employment, it subtly conveys a message that what is natural to blue-collar women is wrong and unacceptable. Rita said, "The language was an obstacle. I think that goes with the issue of publishing and now with the writing." She also noted that in today's marketplace, there has been more emphasis on publishing "conceptual papers." In spite of this marketplace reality, graduate school training often emphasizes quantitative research and writing "technical" or "analytical" papers which focus on specifics and not abstractions. As detailed in a previous chapter, these are exactly the differences which are generally evident in blue-collar homes: a focus on the concrete and an absence of dialog around abstract reasoning. Marcia also blamed academic journals for "misuse of language." She saw publications as "full of jargon" and having a "political application," in that higher education faculty are forced into "jockeying for position and protecting the career they're in" by bowing to publishers' dictates, using a language which is neither direct nor honest, and typically not comfortable for the blue-collar writer.

In the aftermath of rejection of written work which often occurs, Rita recalled her self-doubts: "I think you are questioning your own abilities. Do I belong in this process? Do I belong here? Do I belong there? Not really ..." But she noted that when such challenges occur, she returns to what she knows how to do well: research and teaching. Academic journals thus have limited power of silencing.

The power of language as a system of communication and also as a marker of social class is clear. Language is how we claim voice, or accept silencing. The respondents described situations from their early childhood through their present careers in which differences in language made critical differences to them as individuals from blue-collar backgrounds and as members of an upper-class professional environment.

The New Impostor Syndrome

Pauline Rose Clance, in her book, *The Impostor Phenomenon*[92], described an interesting occurrence of careful self-presentation compounded with self-doubt: "Impostors believe they are intellectual frauds who have attained success because they were at the right place at the right time, knew someone in power, or simply were hard workers—never because they were talented or intelligent or deserved their positions.[93]"

The so-called "impostor phenomenon" suggests that regardless of external evidence of talent and success, victims (Clance's term) of this syndrome are plagued by doubts about their competence and live in fear of failure and/or discovery. Having consistently been top performers, they have an internal need to be "the best" at whatever they do. Clance notes that women in particular are likely to have conflicting feelings about success, fearing it because of the threat of achievement to intimate relationships with men (spouse or father), and the cost of being more successful than significant others in terms of emotional distancing and rejection. This latter factor is especially salient for individuals from lower social class backgrounds[94].

Much of the impostor syndrome, as Clance outlined it, rings true for these respondents. However, in one particular aspect the respondents' self-perceptions seem to conflict with this scenario. They seem quite clear about their own competence; they know they are brighter than most people, more hard-working, and certainly capable of high achievement. The self-doubt experienced by the respondents seems more directly related to their sense of not matching predominant class-based norms in the higher education environment, and to a lesser extent, gendered norms in this setting. The "new" aspect of the impostor syndrome has to do with the extent to which the respondents attempted to modify external aspects of themselves so that others in the higher education environment would perceive them as belonging in that setting.

The research participants reported their perceptions of class-based gaps in expectations of what higher education professionals "look like" versus working-class realities. They recalled numerous instances of trying to fit in by being a "chameleon" and changing with the requirements of the situation or setting. They recounted their attempts to acquire the accouterments of upper-class experiences, such as travel, attire, manners, and a general breadth of experience to which they had not previously been exposed. They also discussed their thoughts on emotional restraints and physical self-control which seemed required in the higher education environment. These sub themes will be discussed in greater detail with supporting evidence in this section.

The previous section described some situations in which the interviewees modified their vocabulary or communication style to match the higher education environment. Pam said that "to make sure that I can relate to people" she had to be "the chameleon." The phenomenon of disguising oneself in some fashion is not new. You will recall how Penny hid her lack of a college degree; after all, in the higher education environment degrees are clearly of utmost value. In her early career, Pat reported "A lack of confidence, even in the face of success." She specifically referred to the impostor syndrome, saying, "This impostor feeling was real prevalent for me as a younger woman … I think I used a lot of corrections to deal with those competence issues." Similar to the Clance description, Pat echoed her recollections of feeling "inadequate or not good enough."

Pat also recognized the pull to respond to the expectations of others. For example, she related how her encounters with other mothers at the college daycare center were often uncomfortable. "The expectation, you know, the kid with the college instructor mom, I'm supposed to be something different than I am. And I show up in my jeans and sneakers and my backpack, like every other mom, and I just don't have stuff that's supposed to go with this education."

The interviewees had many methods of "fitting in;" whether consciously or not. They were bright enough to be able to scan the environment for clues as to prevailing norms. Nancy said, "I was never so over my head that I didn't have context to track what was going on. So whenever something came up, I was a quick enough learner to be able to say, 'Oh, this [is what's expected], I can roll with this punch. And pick it up along the way." She referred to this as "always being able to fudge it."

In such situations where the norm was too distant from her experience to be able to believably fake it, Eileen had a defensive maneuver: "I would [mention] names, and I would say, 'Oh, do you know so-and-so?' And so get the attention off of me, and let's put the attention on somebody else." Avoiding notice was one way of blending into the background with less risk of discovery. Pat used a similar defense in unfamiliar or uncomfortable social situations, "not saying anything, which is typically the way to get through those things."

Karen recalled a business trip on which she traveled with a highly respected and "sophisticated" professor during her graduate school years to a "very, very nice hotel". She said, "I will never forget this trip because … it is true you've got to know what drink to order, and how to behave, and my idea was, if you just shut up and don't say anything it will be OK." In short, she said, "you want to hide ... you want to appear to know what you are doing." She recalled that it felt like "the most uncomfortable trip, because I couldn't succeed here," not knowing the correct ways to behave in such unfamiliar territory. She chose silence as the ultimate hiding place: "It was the trip where I realized, when in doubt, be quiet. It works pretty well." Pat's and Karen's stories, as noted above, may exemplify self-imposed silencing when authentic voice would be too revealing of social class identity and thus unsafe in uncertain social situations.

Linda felt that women from blue-collar backgrounds were easily able to blend into upper-class or other unique environments: "People from working-class backgrounds can play the chameleon role, to use that term, and deal with people from a variety of walks of life, easier than someone who came from a middle-class or an upper-class background."

She added, "I'm not saying you're comfortable, but you can fake it a lot better than someone who's from an upper-class background." Nancy expanded on Linda's comments: "I can charm you. I can make you like me if I need that to be true. In order to get my work done ... I can find some way to connect with you. It's a skill."

Pam mentioned going to college for the first time and understanding that travel, both domestic and international, was commonplace for other incoming freshmen (and certainly faculty). "My two roommates from New York City had just been to Europe, the summer before we started college." Pat also noticed that there were differences between herself and her middle-class male colleagues "that I may not have been exposed to, coming from a blue-collar background." When asked for specifics, she replied, "Travel. A lack of travel and an exposure to things ... I still haven't traveled internationally. Most of my colleagues have ..." For Stephanie, travel is emblematic of the ways in which her life experiences vastly differ from those of her privileged students. She noted, "They've been to so many different countries. Their father owns an airline."

Pat also mentioned some attempts she had made to close that class-based deficiency of breadth of socially-valued experience in other areas. "I want to hit every museum in every city I am in. Because that's sort of a gap. I think that's a class gap. I just wasn't exposed to the arts ..." She continued, "I think I feel a lack of things that middle-class people learn through their contacts and osmosis."

The subject of attire was one which the focus group laughed and joked about, but which was also a serious subject concerning norms and standards in higher education. It began with Linda's shame over the hand-me-downs she, like other respondents, had to wear as a child. Pam recalled, "For me and the working class folk who I know, we didn't talk about brand names growing up. I never knew brand names were important." Charlene added, "I never knew there were any. [laughter]" Pam continued her story in which the rage in college was a particular brand of jeans: "At the time that I was in college, it was Guess jeans; it was all I could do to buy a pair of Guess jeans. I've owned one pair in my whole life, and they were just the thing." She added, "We never talked in those terms when I was growing up."

Conversation about attire in the in-depth interview revived some old and painful memories for Penny. She recalled of her mother, "I found out later that the reason she didn't come to school very much, like to PTA meetings ... was because she never thought she had the clothes to wear. And I just think about some of the stuff and I get so upset, to think that [the college town] is kind of snobbish in that way."

Similarly, Leo shared a story about issues with clothing and the assumed expectations even in surprising educational environments:

> I had a bright teenage girl in a special program for delinquent girls—she had been arrested for prostitution—whose mother wanted her to quit school and go to work to help with the family's financial needs. After several conversations that showed the girl would not prevail, I asked her to bring her mother to see me, perhaps I could persuade her. A long time passed; the girl did not drop out, but the mother did not come either. I finally asked about it. The answer was that the mother was obese and didn't have a proper dress to come to school; she had been saving to buy the fabric so she could make a dress to fit her, so she wouldn't be ashamed. She never did come. The girl finished the semester, possibly under duress from the authorities, but I never saw her again.[95]

Kim acknowledged that, "Yes, I spent a lot of money on a professional wardrobe." She added, "That probably goes to the fact that I'm trying to show that I'm this kind of person." Stephanie described herself as "a fashion dud." She said that her clothes are "definitely not name brands, and my shoes are all awful ..." She noticed that other women "dress better" and "have the nicer hairdo's." She noted that given her current professional position in higher education, "My husband tells me that I should go out and buy a really nice wardrobe. I should be finished, and have the accessories." In reference to what she called her "horrible wardrobe", she added, "My husband says to me, 'I can't believe you go out and teach like this.'" One of the qualities she appreciated in her current friends was that "they don't have to be wearing the nicest things." However, she saw a connection between appearance and social class: "I think it's almost like a presence

... sometimes it's very easy to tell people of means. Their whole persona, their polish—and I am extremely unpolished. I think it's easy for people to tell that I come from hard-working, regular America.... I don't wear a lot of makeup. I don't have manicures."

In a recent situation, Pam combined her frugal blue-collar roots with her current brand-name consciousness: "I go to work dressed in my Talbots dress, that I got for 57 dollars, originally 173 dollars [laughter]." Jennifer reported similar cost-consciousness regarding attire: "I just went shopping last week. I got a couple skirts for three and four dollars [laughs] ... I wouldn't buy a suit because it was expensive and a brand name, I'd buy it because it would be on sale, and it looked expensive ..."

Linda noted that upscale attire could create barriers with students from lower socioeconomic backgrounds. "If I dressed like I do at a conference or at [administrators] meetings, in [my college town] it would be a barrier. It would create a class barrier ... because clothes reflect money to some folks." For her to dress too differently from her clientele would cause some resentment. Likewise, Penny said, "I deliberately don't wear 'power suits', because I think that would turn [people] off."

Rita saw modes of dress less a sign of class for her, but rather a sign of culture. For example, she said that she likes "tropical colors" and a distinctive style of dress which she sees as emblematic of her Hispanic background. She acknowledged, however, that there was a certain unspoken dress code, especially for special events sponsored by her workplace.

Marcia demonstrated some annoyance with and resistance to norms for dress in her job. She said, "I know the importance of that [in this institution]. I know that we are expected to dress in a certain way ... walking the walk in those little heels and those nice looking suits."

For most faculty members, like Sharon, attire did not carry such weight: "I work in an environment where I don't have to be wearing a power suit to work." She added, "I'm not a particularly materialistic person," suggesting that undue attention to attire may be a sign of conspicuous and unnecessary consumption. She criticized male administrators at her institution who she accused of deception, "I do see them in their lovely suits, perpetrating deceit."

Manners were also the topic of some discussion in the focus group and repeated in the individual interviews. Eileen sheepishly admitted, "I drink out of my cereal bowl, too. And soup bowls. And when I do that, I shake people up." Kim laughingly recalled that she had to learn "that girls don't drink beers out of bottles ... I didn't know that!" Pat acknowledged, "There are social skills that I don't have, but being the [odd] child sort of helped me in that respect, because I got comfortable being the outsider, the person on the fringe, the one that doesn't fit in. I think I do that a little in terms of my identity on the job."

Stephanie called herself "a social moron." She said that her mother tried to teach her proper etiquette, but she was busy being a "tomboy". She said, "I should read the manners books because being in [this profession], you wouldn't believe how many events you have to go to, [and] I'm looking at the silverware going, 'Oh my God!' And probably because it's a part of my job, I will have to go learn about manners." She added, "It's something I'm not all that comfortable with, and I think I'm going to have to gain a comfort level with it, because there are some expectations that come along with being a [university] professor."

Penny recalled that although her family was very poor, her mother tried to teach her good manners. She, also, was busy being a "tomboy" and paid little attention at the time. In addition to good table manners, she insisted "that you were always clean, soap and water, cheap, [laughs] you never have to be dirty ... and try to take care of your teeth." Although she now has dentures, Penny says it doesn't bother her as a potential sign of her social class background, although "certainly [bad] teeth is one way of showing that you didn't have money." However, she acknowledged, "that's another defense mechanism that I've learned; people can only tease you about something if they think it's going to bother you, so I just pretend [it doesn't]." She added, wistfully, "Sometimes I think I live this whole life of pretend."

Even the topic of cigarette smoking found connections with social class background. Penny and Pat noted that they were likely to smoke (or had smoked) with blue-collar friends; as Pat recalled, "I think I smoked for years past when it was healthy for me, because it kept me in that sort of working-class place out on the porch with women. There's sort of a class thing that goes on with that." Penny said, "I think low socioeconomic or lower-class people still smoke more …"

An important sub-theme was that of restraint, emotional and physical. It came up first in the focus group interview, when Pam said to Charlene, "I associate this with a class thing. You know, rich people don't laugh loud. And Charlene laughs loud. And I laugh loud. Have you ever noticed that in a room? The wealthy don't laugh loud." Linda felt that one asset to coming from a blue-collar background was, "You're able to laugh a lot more." Pat also noted, in speaking of a friend, "She thinks that I am probably one of the funnier people that she's ever met, because I don't cover my feelings." There was a definite perception that people from upper-class backgrounds are not having a good time, are not able to express joy without restraint.

You will recall that Kim's male superior accused her of "getting emotional" when she disagreed with him and the volume of her voice increased. She said, "When I feel very strongly on a particular topic, I don't hold back." This is an example of how the expression of anger is discouraged in the higher education environment. Kim later said that she has had to learn "… how to be diplomatic. And how not to show a lot of emotion. How to be assertive, yet not aggressive."

At the same time, recalling the punitive attitude of Rita's institution when she needed to devote time to mourning her father's death, there was some subtext that blue-collar and/or ethnic cultures grieve too strongly, and for too long; in contrast then, it is logical to wonder if the emotional restraint of joy which characterized these perceptions of upper-class persons translates into an equal restraint upon sorrow.

Rita also related individual restraint to control of behavior. She said, "I really try to focus on my behavior … what's appropriate, what's inappropriate. So I set for myself stronger limitations and guidelines. You will be a professional. You make sure you're acting as a professional, even though some professional over there acts like a fool." She concluded, "So it's that kind of control that I set for myself..... I will watch my step." She related this need for control to job security; for example, at the faculty cocktail party, "[I'm] not going to drink more than two drinks because these are not your friends." She felt that if she made a mistake, even one which might be overlooked in another faculty member, "I'd lose my job."

There is a connection between this sub theme of restraint and concerns the respondents voiced regarding ethics in higher education. Pat said, "I don't have the kind of pretensions you need to take care of yourself in vicious organizations." This echoed the deeper meaning of remarks from the previous section on language, such as "talking the talk," being concerned about image, pretentiousness, and dishonesty in academe. Sharon, as previously noted, connected polished external appearances with internal deception; a metaphorical wolf in sheep's clothing. Stephanie earlier mentioned the "persona" of a polished individual; Penny noted some more pejorative aspects of "persona": "I don't have this professional persona that other administrators have. I don't want to put on airs of any kind." Susan also resisted adoption of a different persona; "If I kept up with the persona, the image of, or trying to please everybody, I was going to tire very, very quickly."

Although the interviewees seemed to have some distaste for the perceived emotional restraint of upper-class people, there were numerous stories of "aloofness" among the respondents. This may be connected to the sub theme of silencing which was previously noted. Pat said, "I still stand apart from people. I don't know if that's a class defense." She reported that people have at times asked her, "Why do you do that? Why do you hang out on the edges, instead of mix with people?" She responded that she is uncomfortable with her social skills, and added, "I would rather back off. I think that's a class problem." Her professional comfort zone is in "staying back and being the marginal one." Similarly, Jennifer said, "We have a faculty dining room here and I never eat lunch there." She felt uncomfortable there, and added, "I'm not going to pretend to be any different [from myself] because I'm with [the faculty]." She also stated, "that's their problem and that's not mine if I don't fit in." The phenomenon of not fitting in—in many places—is explored in depth in the next section of this chapter.

Playing the impostor game was not restricted to one's professional life within the institution. As Charlene pointed out, membership in professional organizations also has required that "I have to play chameleon." She claimed that, "There are so many times when I have been shut out of conversations, or shut out of situations because I'm at the community colleges." And even at community-college-specific organizations, she recognized that the administrators from upper-class backgrounds are not necessarily going to accept or associate with her because of her social class background.

The women I interviewed were successful impostors; that is, they typically reported, as Nancy did, that "a lot of people assume otherwise"; that is, their colleagues assumed that they were from middle- or upper-class social backgrounds. Kim said of her colleagues' perceptions of her social class background, "I don't think there's anything visually they see. In fact they probably think the opposite, that I come from a middle-class family." Nancy also noted repercussions from this guise. She recalled a colleague who recently "referred to me behind my back, as the Princess. And I thought, 'Wow, if she only knew.'" She concluded, "I really fool people ... it's not intentional at all." However, I would argue that long years of actively blending in with prevailing upper-class norms in education, particularly from high school and beyond, remove the effort from conscious awareness and bury it in the subconscious mind where it is less troubling in terms of identity and self-esteem issues. With regard to the New York accent which is not apparent to most ears, Susan said, "I don't do anything consciously, not to talk that way, but maybe I do and I just don't realize it."

In conclusion, the women I interviewed related an ability to function effectively in two worlds. As Linda said of her blue-collar background, "That whole culture was just part of me." But she, like the others, was able to adapt to the culture of higher education, a culture that was distinctly different from that of her youth. The class-based variations were not restricted to superficialities of attire and manners, but to an underlying judgment of those superficial signs of appearance and behavior as carrying the weight of substantive differences in character. Social skills were not just meaningless trivia, but emblems, like language, of social class and individual worth. These "new" impostors have worked hard to achieve their professional positions, and recognize that they deserve to hold them; however, they also recognize that the superficialities of the environment must also be attended to as symbols of membership in that realm.

The Lone(ly) Ranger

In American culture, one of our popular television heroes of yesteryear was the Lone Ranger, a masked man on a white horse who vanquished villains and rode off in solitude into the happy ending. The absence of a comparable heroine is not surprising, given the pervasiveness of male dominance in our history. The research participants in this study bore a strong resemblance to the aforementioned hero in their self-perceptions of different-ness and identities formed around their marginality in the family and in educational settings. In spite of or because of this sense of other-ness, the interviewees developed personal traits such as independence and assertiveness which allowed them to be successful. Their different-ness was sometimes experienced as isolation and loneliness in both personal and professional lives; they sometimes maintained emotional distance from others purposely as well. Their marginal identity, accompanied by class-based values, made them reject the hierarchies they found in the higher education setting, as well as the pretensions they saw in colleagues. Their class background also translated into difficulty relating to students from privileged backgrounds, both in their own educational histories and as workers in higher education. The interrelationships among these components are explored here in greater depth.

Each interview revealed a commonality among the respondents; each woman's identity had been formed around other-ness. They told stories of being identified as "different" in their family from early in life. This followed in college, when they felt different from their peers, and in graduate school as well. In their professional lives, the solitary nature of their pursuits appeared repeatedly.

Not only were they identified as different, and identified themselves as such, but they demonstrated a resistance to some of the prevailing norms of their immediate surroundings and developed the personal traits which enabled them to be proactive against or in spite of these norms. These traits included independence, assertiveness, and the ability and willingness to act as advocates for themselves, even when no-one else could or would. As Penny said, "I was fairly independent and I didn't ask for help. I still don't." Susan described the ways in which she differed from other members of her family: "They knew I was different ... I was a little bit more outgoing ... I was much more assertive ... I was much more independent ..."

In the face of some dismal family situations, including alcoholism, divorce, and gender bias, or simple lack of encouragement to thrive, their resiliency and self-determination were undoubtedly keys to their success. They often reported making key life decisions on their own, independent of input from family or in the virtual absence of the same. At the same time, while fathers were often negative influences in the lives of the respondents, most of these women had mothers who played key roles in supporting and encouraging them, or at the least modeling perseverance, hard work, and innate intelligence. This somehow made their other-ness acceptable and even a desirable feature.

The following are some revealing quotes which underscore the interviewees' self-identification as marginal:

—On childhood experiences:

Linda: It was pretty much a lonely childhood ...

Nancy: I was an anomaly in my family ...

Pat: [I was] hero-child-daughter. I was the smart one.

Pat: I'm the odd one.

Jennifer: I was always a loner. I felt like I didn't fit in.

Jennifer: I don't feel like I belong with my family.

Sharon: I didn't really form any friendships.

Stephanie: I was a big-time loner ...

Stephanie: [I felt] like I wasn't good enough with peers.

Karen: I never have felt like I quite belonged.

Rita: I was the only one [who went to college].

Rita: I was the only Hispanic [in my neighborhood].

Marcia: I was a social non-entity in high school.

Susan: I was very different from my [siblings].

—On college:

Charlene: I'm the only person in my family to ever go to college.

Nancy: I'm the only one of five [to go to college].

Pam: .. you don't know anyone [in college]

Pat: I went alone. I knew nobody there.

Pat: I was one female student out of a class of 15 guys.

Jennifer: I missed out a lot on the fun..

Sharon:[I thought], 'I really don't want to be with these people.'

Rita: [The students said] 'You're the pioneer.'

Rita: (on writing a dissertation) Leave me alone.

Rita: The Ph.D. creates an isolation.

—On professional colleagues:

Charlene: I just didn't fit.

Pat: I was lonely … it is mostly men …

Pat: I feel different than most of my colleagues.

Pat: [I'm] the marginal one.

Jennifer: I feel like I don't belong there …

Sharon: Their values [are] different from mine.

Stephanie: It's a sense that I don't belong.

Karen: I never feel I belong.

Rita: I'm a scapegoat.

Rita: These are not your friends.

Marcia: I was by myself.

Marcia: I have no professional colleagues on the staff here.

Penny: I just never feel as though I quite belong.

Kim: There are instances when I feel that I shouldn't be there.

The directness of these quotes makes an unmistakable statement about the isolation, alienation, and disconnection which these women feel. However, taking on the role of "outsider" can also open up possibilities for self-evolution and professional risk which might not be available to those who cling to "insider" identities. Nancy recalled a situation early in her career when she acted as a consultant to a group who, she felt, perceived her as a "friendly alien." She could play the role of the outside expert, "And I didn't really have to go out on a limb in terms of class" in order to blend into the environment, because there was a built-in expectation—or even requirement—that she would be different.

Charlene and Pam noted their disregard for institutional hierarchies. Pam said, "I don't pay much attention to the hierarchy … I'm as likely to sit next to the president at lunch and say hello, and yuk it up a little bit, as I am anybody else …" Charlene noted that colleagues call her "irreverent" because, "I don't put people into these sort of pyramids of belonging, somebody above somebody else. I don't understand this hierarchical ladder…. it's not the context or the reality that I grew up in." Pat also noted of her hometown, "We didn't have class boundaries."

The concept of superior-inferior relationships is distasteful and uncomfortable to many women, so some respondents chose to disregard it, while others actively rejected it. By rejecting it, they also refused its potential rejection of them. Charlene continued, "[Hierarchy] doesn't exist in the [working class] community. You know, everybody's sort of from the same place. And anybody that's not, is the other. And you know you're never going to be there. You're never going to be part of the other; you're never going to be part of that class."

A similar sub theme was a rejection of perceived cruelty, superficiality, hypocrisy, and manipulativeness in professional colleagues. Pat said, "The things that I saw that the faculty did, I thought were awful! They were phony and they were yucky, and I couldn't do them, and I didn't want to do them!" She explained further that they "pulled rank on people, put people down." Stephanie also reported a feeling that "people are getting things that don't deserve it." That is, that colleagues from higher social-class backgrounds do not have to earn their rewards, they simply get them. Penny recalled her anger at hypocrisy in the social and professional environment: "Hypocrisy has been something I've just never been able to abide, and still can't." She has felt that this is a problem in higher education, but one which she has felt comfortable standing up to.

Rita reported feeling exploited by the institution and her colleagues: "They were just using me." There was a distinct mistrust in her professional relationships; she said that she has had to be "very selective with who you talk to, who you are going to confide with." This mistrust was echoed by Marcia, who saw in the politics of her professional environment "a patent dishonesty to what they do."

Like other respondents, Jennifer rejected pretension in the workplace: "I'm not going to pretend to be any different [than I am] because I'm sitting having lunch with the dean of whatever division ..." At a different level, Stephanie related a story (complete with disdainful voice in imitation of the speaker) in which a female colleague in her department advised her on how to get tenure:

> [She said], 'Well, the only way you are going to get tenure is if you hire a staff. You have to have a staff. That's how I got tenure, I had a staff.' And I'm like, a staff?! What the heck is she talking about? ... But she had a cook. She had an errand person. She had a full-time nanny. Even though this is a decent salary, we could never afford that!

She concluded, "It's just something that's so completely foreign to me." At the same time, however, a note of loneliness crept into her voice as she talked about a feeling of "not belonging" in her professional environment: "It's a sense of, is there anyone who really understands me?" Her colleagues' experiences are so vastly different, that it seemed unlikely to her that they could understand her.

A prior section in this chapter reflected on the role of publishing in the professional lives of women faculty; the pressure to conduct research and to write for publication also can have an isolating effect. As Rita said, "You remove yourself to a point, where you just totally remove yourself. You have to remove." She continued, "You have to be very careful with that." Rita clearly saw a danger in too great a degree of professional isolation.

Another aspect of the interviewees' careers which has reinforced different-ness was their difficulty relating to students who came from advantaged backgrounds. Sharon said, "I don't take education for granted. I was always astonished to see students who were just kind of going through the motions." She continued, "... for them it's just kind of a re-acquisition of what their parents already have. It's just kind of more of the same. And they don't really know why they're doing it ..." Stephanie's experience at a prestigious institution was very similar:

> That's the one thing I have a problem with here, being a teacher at [Ivy U.]. My students, most of their parents own some kind of company, or multiple hotels, or whatever. And to see the way that they look at their education. It's handed to them on a platter. The parents paid for it. And the way they look at work is really hard for me. Because with [my] kind of upbringing, I definitely feel like I value money and work and education.

Stephanie felt that the students take for granted something for which she and her family had to toil and sacrifice. "There are a few students that I do get annoyed with," she said, "They are the students who just have it so well off, and just don't have an appreciation for what they have. And flaunt it or take it for granted." Karen added, "There's a sense of privilege that some of our students have, that I wish they didn't have ... an inability to think of a world that is less privileged than the one that they came from. They just think that's the way it is everywhere." She reported trying to raise their class consciousness in an instructional setting and encouraging discussion of public assistance: "I talk a little about welfare policy, and our students just can't understand it. They can't understand why somebody doesn't have a job."

Marcia, as cited earlier, recalled the friction she felt as an instructor at a college populated by students from upper-class backgrounds. She left the institution, grateful that in her frustration with attitudes of privilege and ignorance of poverty, "Murder had not been done."

Pam said, "I could not relate to their experience at all." She also noted, with considerable agitation, that it angers her to be considered "privileged" simply because she is Caucasian, in comparison with students of color at her institution who often come from wealthy families:

> For many of the targeted groups who we talk about, specifically students of color, and international students, specifically of color, many of the students who I have known who are African-American or Asian, ... I'm consistently compared to as privileged by virtue of the fact that I am white, but most of those students ... have been far better off than me socioeconomically.

Her confusion, as she described it, has to do with "when privilege and oppression sort of sit in the same body." She added, "it doesn't feel like a fit. It feels like I want to throw up."

On the other hand, those who worked with students from lower social-class backgrounds reported positive relationships and professional satisfaction in working with these groups. Marcia, whose experience at a private college had been so miserable, felt much more comfortable teaching students at a public institution. "I got along very well," she recalled, with the students whose backgrounds were more like her own. Even at the private research university, Stephanie noted her enjoyment of being "a role model" for students who, in that setting, were "misfits". She said, "There's a lot more of a bond and a sympathy and an understanding level for students who are the misfits here. We identify very easily, and I feel for them, because I see myself." She was happy to self-disclose some of her own history to these select students, so that they would know that, "Things aren't going to be that rainbow road for everybody, and it's OK." Stephanie's story also revealed some class conflict between students at her institution; she noted that there are students "who just do not feel comfortable with the display of wealth" which may consist of driving expensive cars versus inexpensive used ones, and tales of travel told in class.

Karen also reported that at her top-tier institution, "We have some students who come here, and this is such a change for them, such a different kind of place for them, and it's hard." She added, "there's a certain kind of empathy for students who are having adjustment problems, that maybe you don't have so much, if you didn't see that."

It is relevant here to again mention Stephanie's recollections regarding the "wall" she had built up around herself. Maintaining an emotional distance was also part of Pat's experience, one which carried over into her professional life. She expressed a sentiment that one of the positive aspects of teaching is the turnover of students which happens naturally each semester: "Every three months I get another batch, and you can keep a certain amount of emotional distance." You will recall that Pat earlier mentioned a certain "aloofness" which is habitual for her in both professional and social situations; both of these forms of detachment may represent a protective defense mechanism learned early in life.

Jennifer also maintained a distance from colleagues in her professional life by declining to dine in the faculty dining room. In addition, she said, "People I work with professionally, they don't know me very personally or know my background." She later added, "I think other people might not like me, or may not like being around me, 'cause I'm myself, I'm not going to pretend ..." She concluded, "[I] just don't have a lot in common" with other professionals at the college.

Penny said, "I guess I've almost always felt as though I didn't belong." She continued, "I just always feel as though I don't quite fit in ... I don't want to get too close to people, because I don't want them to hurt me. If I'm not too close, then they can't hurt me ... That's been a serious problem in my personal relationships. My independence." Although Penny and Stephanie are dissimilar in many other ways—one is faculty and the other an administrator, one just beginning her career and one near the end of it, one with a Ph.D. and one without a college degree—the common feeling which they shared is one of extreme vulnerability and a fierce independence designed to protect themselves from emotional harm. In their reasoning, it appeared that closeness is interpreted as dependence—too risky a position—while distance allows for independence and thus safety.

Many of these women reported a lonely social life, with few friends. Sharon voiced a sentiment which many seemed to share: "I don't have that many really close friends ... I'm not somebody who feels that she has to have a lot of close friends to function or survive. I think friendship is an unusual thing." Pat said, "I haven't pursued friendships for the most part." She later added that "I don't seem to have a lot in common with [other single women with children], they are ten years younger than me, and invariably have clerical jobs somewhere." Jennifer also noted that in college, while other students "had a lot of friends ... I didn't have that ..." For her, this was partly a function of time restrictions; she was working long hours as well as being a full-time student. However, I would also argue that it was at least in part a personal preference which was developing; one which preferred alone-ness over the risk of social relationships.

Jennifer spoke about her distance from people both in the professional setting and outside: "I don't really have someone to talk to, or a close friend that I talk to about personal things, or anything outside of work at all." Stephanie likewise related few close social ties. "I developed a little bit of a hard exterior, and I don't think, really let too many people get very close to me. I don't have a lot of friends. I have very few to no friends."

Marcia, in discussing a gradual distancing from college friends, said, "They have had normal lives. I haven't really ..." She told about her feelings of discomfort and lack of commonality because most of them are married with children, and she is unmarried and does not have children. She further noted, "There is certainly a kind of social confidence that I've never had." Between being unmarried, which she has labeled as abnormal in view of society's norms, and this lack of ease in social interaction, Marcia could easily be described as a loner. She said, "I've never belonged socially, ever."

Penny, who has stayed in her hometown for the duration of her professional life, has been able to maintain contact with high school friends. Recalling her distaste for hypocrisy, she also said of her friends, "They don't have an inflated view of who they are ... and they don't like hypocrisy either." This is obviously in reaction to the "snobbish" nature of the college town in which they live.

Rita noted with regret that she has few friends from her home any more; she blames herself. She stated that in her hometown, "There's no stimulation for me. So with my friends that are now working-class friends, there's that gap again. So I just bring myself down. I never expect them, or criticize them. I'm the one that's wrong here." In further discussing the highly technical world in which she now functions, in comparison with the lack of "outside stimulation" of her hometown environment, she reiterated that, "You're the only one." The lack of commonality was clear.

Other-ness has become a comfortable position, marginality a positive experience. Nancy said, "I understand different-ness, and I'm self-aware about it ..." This allowed her to relate well to a variety of people. Pat said, "I got comfortable being the outsider, the person on the fringe, the one that doesn't fit in." She continued, "You just sort of get comfortable as the odd guy out." Pat expressed a positive attitude about her marginality; "I knew I was a different kind of person [than the other faculty]." Similarly, Rita said of her blue-collar background, "It has made me the person I am today." Jennifer said, "I was always more of a loner. Just doing what I believed in, rather than being influenced by others." Her comments reflected a negative judgment about group-ness; a fear of the crowd mentality that goes along with belonging.

In conclusion, I refer again to Rita's comments, previously cited, in relation to the loneliness that comes with being in college, first as a student and then as a professional. As she said, achievement at an advanced level in higher education "is an isolating thing. It can also be intimidating to other people. You're culturally isolated, educationally isolated, professionally isolated."

Even when respondents reported being popular in high school, like Penny and Stephanie, they still reported social and professional isolation in their current lives. Why did they arrive at the same destination as those who reported being social misfits in their early lives, such as Jennifer and Marcia? Was it a question of personal transformation, or of professional location and social (dis)location?

One thing can be concluded with certainly; these women lead solitary professional lives and relatively limited social lives. Is this a reflection of increasing isolation in the larger society? Or is it possible that they exist in a transitional social location between the world of their roots and that of their current professional identities, no longer belonging in the former, and not willing to fully embrace the latter? Are they living, as Al Lubrano says, in Limbo?[96]

It also seemed clear that, although they were currently living lives of relative isolation, these women cared deeply about connection with others. Disconnection was their choice only because superficial connection was not acceptable or desirable.

The Undiscussable Nature of Class

In the United States, the dominant ideology insists that every citizen is equal. It is a democracy, a meritocracy, a veritable level playing field where every person can attain his or her full potential through hard work and talent. Why, then, do so many people from lower social-class backgrounds in the United States find that, for them, it is not so? Why is this disjuncture of espoused cultural values and indisputable facts-on-the-ground not discussed? It appeared that other-ness is not acceptable in a democratic society which claims to celebrate equality, and thus it is not discussed—as if it does not exist.

In the individual interviews, the undiscussability of social class in the higher education setting appeared repeatedly. The interviewees noted that the topic of social class does not typically arise in this environment. When it does come up, it is discussed in the abstract, depersonalized, as an academic sub-specialty. The perception of the women I interviewed was that there appears to be no language to discuss class issues among colleagues or in the classroom. Their comments suggested that although they clearly see the existence of social stratification in American culture, there is a pervasive and insistent denial of real social class differences and of class-based tensions in higher education.

Pam said in the focus group interview, "people don't talk about class." Charlene replied, "That's very true." To which Pam responded, "And it's hard not to talk about it." Eileen went on to say that in her experience in academe, class was not talked about except in abstract academic terms. She said, "It just never came up in conversation." She said that what is left outstanding is "a lot of questions of class ..." In terms of her Irish-immigrant blue-collar background, and a larger view on professions in the United States, she said, "Where you're placed, [in addition to social class] is not based on skills, but who you are, your heritage and color."

Pam related an experience where a friend of hers assumed that the poverty he saw in the south was a function of the inhabitants' color. She asked, "Or is it a function of class, that no one talks about?" She went on, "It seems really to be the base of everything, you know, to be able to assign people to these classes ..."

Pat's comfort level in discussing class issues has become part of her professional role; she said that as a faculty member in the social sciences, "Class analysis is part of what I do." The abstraction of this sort of analysis perhaps decreased the painful nature of it. She concluded, "That is part of how I intellectually deal with our stratification system."

I asked the individual interviewees if the topic of social class ever came up in conversation with professional colleagues. Here is a sample of the responses to that question:

Jennifer: No, never.

Sharon: Ah, no. Certainly not.

Stephanie: It's like a non-discussible.

Karen: In the abstract.

Rita: No.

A few respondents answered the question by addressing the meaning of or existence of "professional colleagues" and thus did not address the substance of the question. Kim, the only respondent who answered in the affirmative, is in a role in a community college setting which promotes the idea of self-disclosure in order to connect with disadvantaged students, and this may explain the uniqueness (in this group) of her response. However, as previously cited, Kim noted that her colleagues were "surprised" to learn of her social class background, and had assumed otherwise.

Sharon summarized this dilemma of undiscussability quite nicely:

> My sense is that class is an issue that a lot of people have blipped out ... Even though you would think class issues might be noticed by various people who have done feminist readings, they haven't. It's almost as if the people in the United States want to be blind to class. They don't really have a way of deciding how class might affect issues about race and gender. And they don't have an easily available vocabulary for talking about those issues. And they're not encouraged to talk about it.

Sharon noted that her students have had great difficulty in thinking and talking about social class issues. They seemed quite satisfied to accept the superficial media images of equality and meritocracy without acknowledging nor examining class conflict issues. She recalled a day when she tried to encourage such dialog in the classroom: "It was clearly very difficult for them because they don't talk about feminism and women's issues and they *really* don't talk about class issues" (her emphasis).

I asked Rita what she thought her colleagues would think if the subject of her social class background did come up in conversation, since she had said that it did not. She replied, "They are supposed to be empathetic being in [a social science field], they should be empathetic. They should understand struggles and issues [about] social class." I pressed her for more, repeating her words, "'supposed to'—what about that?" to which she responded, "That's why I guess maybe it never comes up." There was a clear sense that if the topic arose, even colleagues who were trained in the theoretical aspects of class and social stratification would not understand the true lived experience of it, would not empathize, and thus it was not a safe topic.

In summary, it seems clear that the respondents' perception was that we do not have a language to discuss class issues, and the society as a whole seems to deny the existence of social stratification or of frictions which occur based on such classification.

Members of the Club

Our society values membership, but my research suggests that "belonging" in colleges and universities, both for students and professionals, is restricted and defined along lines of both gender and social class. Thus not belonging, like other-ness, creates a dual marginality, paradoxically based on the dual marginality of being female and from a lower social-class background. Dual marginality may also be understood in the sense of non-belonging in two classes; being alienated from the class of one's origins, and that of one's current social location based on education, occupational prestige, and income. Marginality and an apolitical stance taken by many of the interviewees in their work settings were also a basis for exclusion from membership in the "club" of academe.

The reader will recall that Sharon earlier talked about her experience as a doctoral student at a very prestigious Ivy League institution, and called it "an upper class boys' club." When we deconstruct that phrase into its component parts of social class, gender, and the higher education setting, it is easy to see why a sense of belonging is denied someone who is from a blue-collar background (not upper class), female (not male), and does not meet the criteria for the underlying component of membership or centrality. A female academic from the lower social classes is, in fact, the antithesis of its membership. However, membership in such a "club" is highly socially valued because of its related social class status components: advanced education, elite occupation, and presumably considerable financial rewards.

Stephanie talked about the disadvantage of being from a blue-collar background in terms of striving to reach her educational and professional goals: "You've got to work twice as hard as everybody else. You just do. You don't have the network. You don't have the connections. You don't have things handed to you. It's got to be purely on performance, if you're going to make it, so you'd better be good."

A number of respondents commented on the political dimensions of higher education; they noted their lack of connections and their distaste for "using" contacts. They disliked feeling "used" or exploited by the organization, so it was unlikely that they would feel comfortable in using others for political/professional gain. Regardless of their distaste for it, they recognized how ignorance of institutional politics had increased their struggles. At the same time, however, they declined to become versed in political strategizing for their own benefit. Membership in this particular highly political club perhaps reminded them of their own exclusion; to gain "insider" status might put them in the position of excluding others from membership, not an enviable position or acceptable option for these women.

In summary, then, membership was perceived by the respondents as an ambiguous concept. In terms of the higher education environment, membership was desirable; however, such membership constituted a betrayal of their gender and social class roots because of its traditional exclusion of women and of individuals from lower social-class backgrounds.

When we return to the idea of the master-servant duality, here we see that although these individuals exhibited all the meritocratic qualities for success—talent, effort, and motivation—and had earned a higher rung on the occupational status ladder, they were still excluded from full membership and status of the masters. The rigidity of social class rules is made clear through these stories.

PART IV

Action: The soul of
advocacy

8

Proactivity

For over ten years, I have been giving presentations and workshops on the topic of social class issues in education and the helping professions. Much of the information I share with attendees at these events is contained in this book. As I initially told the stories of my interviewees and others, including my own story, the people with whom I was speaking seemed to slowly deflate. They visibly sank in their seats as they grasped the full implications of the cumulative disadvantage which society heaps upon the working class, and on children in particular. My workshop evaluations would say things like, "I'm really glad I came today. This is great information. I had no idea. Now I feel really depressed."

As a budding scholar, I resisted the temptation to tell people what they should do to change the world. Rather, my role as an academic purist was to only describe my research findings, not to take that frightening leap into providing a prescription or remedy. However, I didn't like the outcome that I was getting. I often spent three or four hours in a workshop convincing people of the enormity of the problem of social class discrimination in our culture, and once they were persuaded, I left them standing at the altar in a state of confusion and depression. I have learned to change this outcome by doing two things: I tell the audience at the beginning and end of the presentation that one person can make a difference, and I truly believe that. And, I now include recommendations for action.

You are now a person who is aware of the reality of social class discrimination. Paulo Freire referred to this as *conscientization*: "Conscientization refers to the process in which men [sic], not as recipients, but as knowing subjects, achieve a deepening awareness both of the socio-cultural reality which shapes their lives and of their capacity to transform that reality."[97] Awareness represents an important initial shift in perception; an awareness, as I suggested earlier, that the Emperor has no clothes. However, as Freire suggests and as I discovered in the process of presenting on this topic, awareness is not enough. The first step is *awareness*; the second step is *action*. As the Dalai Lama said, "It is not enough to be compassionate. You must act." Both awareness without action, and action without awareness, result in no change. The former is simple insight and remains locked within you. The latter translates to thrashing about with no particular goal or purpose.

Through my own experience, as well as ideas of colleagues and workshop participants, I have some plans to share with you towards action. Before you even consider action, let me remind you that one person *can* make a difference, and you may be that one person in the life of someone you know, or for a series of persons you don't even know yet. Most people can recall one person early in their life who made a difference. Sometimes they recall a very negative interaction, but often there is one outstanding comment or action that transformed the individual's ideas about what might be possible in their life. As K. Patricia Cross said, "In the final analysis, the task of the excellent teacher is to stimulate 'apparently ordinary' people to unusual effort. The tough problem is not in identifying winners: it is in making winners out of ordinary people. That, after all, is the overwhelming purpose of education. Yet historically, in most of the periods emphasizing excellence, education has reverted to selecting winners rather than creating them."[98] Are *you* someone who could help to create a winner?

The next step would be to start with an honest examination of yourself and your own practices. Whether you're a teacher, school administrator, college admissions counselor, financial aid officer, career counselor, nurse, or other helping professional, you may want to reflect upon your own underlying thoughts and feelings about social class, and also to seek feedback on your own practices with regard to potential class bias. This is, in fact, a huge undertaking for most people. The next chapter goes into a little more detail about a safe way to do this. When you're pretty certain that you've identified and eliminated any unintentional prejudice and discriminatory practices in your own work, then you're ready to work with others.

The next step is to define your target population. With whom do you work? Who are the individuals who are negatively affected by class discrimination, and who has the power to equalize opportunity structures? Who do you want to change? What are the practices that need modification? What is a safe, proactive way to approach this group? Are you able to identify specific behaviors that you find problematic, and to describe in detail the negative outcomes associated with those behaviors? Do you have a specific preferred behavior that you can suggest, so the problematic behavior is not replaced with an equally problematic one?

Assuming that you're able to get to this point, and perhaps to work directly with students, patients, or other constituents who come from lower social-class backgrounds, here are some specific suggestions that have worked for me and for others:

1. Escape the "present" orientation; when possible, talk *future* with students. They are used to being given explicit or implicit messages that they should stay in their place or at least not to aim too high. Low expectations result in low achievement. Encourage them to describe their dreams in full detail, and allow them to imagine that they might reach their dreams. They can shoot for the stars, or they may choose not to; but be sure to let *them* make the real decisions. It is a mistake to try to protect someone from failure if they reach too high. That's their right.

2. Encourage students with *concrete* truths about them and their potential. There was an era in which psychologists seemed to believe that by simply telling children they were good, wonderful, people, that the children would develop positive self-esteem. It didn't really work, for the same reason that your English teacher told you not to use the word "nice" since it is so vague as to be meaningless. Flesh it out. If Joanie is getting 90's on all her math tests, then point that specific fact out to her as the reason you believe she's good in math. If Bob's English teacher says his last paper was imaginative and full of rich metaphor, tell him those are the reasons you know he's a good writer. "You're a good student" isn't good enough.

3. Likewise, kindness isn't enough. Having good intentions is like the Poppy Queen in my town riding around in an open automobile during the July 4th parade. She looks nice, but so what? What is it all for? Provide personalized *information* to the student about careers, strategies for academic success, graduate schools, networking for employment, etc. When I say *personalized*, I mean that the generic information that is provided to *all* students may not fit *this* student in particular. Take the time and invest the effort in finding and providing information that is specific to this person's interests, talents, and abilities. This doesn't mean doing all the work for him or her; rather, it means doing a sufficient amount of background work to provide them with a foundation of data that connects to a larger web of information.

So, for example, if the student is interested in careers in medicine, you wouldn't present only information on the MCAT (Medical College Admission Test), nor only on nursing school for LPNs (licensed practical nurse), but perhaps a broad array of career and educational information about careers in medicine that s/he could then further investigate.

4. Eliminate unnecessary costs. As a college faculty member, I am frequently astounded at the cost of textbooks. Some professors require three or four textbooks, costing upwards of $250 per course. This is unaffordable for many students from poverty backgrounds; in fact, some students try to struggle along without course texts, which puts them at a distinct disadvantage in the classroom and in terms of optimal learning outcomes. If you're a teacher, put required course readings on library reserve so purchase is not required.

   Likewise, there are many extracurricular activities in Kindergarten through 12th grade that carry considerable extra cost to the family. For example, a few years ago my son's school promoted a special trip for members of the middle school band. The required deposit alone was over $300 and the total cost exceeded $700. There was some very small print about needy families and the possibility of applying for scholarship funds. Many families on limited budgets will not even attempt to get support for these kind of enrichment activities. They are subject to society's shaming already; it is unlikely they will submit themselves to additional humiliation of seeking financial assistance for their child. If your school or other organization can't afford to underwrite the special extra-cost activity, either don't offer it, or plan fundraising activities so that every child can attend regardless of financial means.

   The bottom line here: don't charge fees for events if possible because you will automatically be excluding a certain segment of the population. This additional marginalization is not helpful in creating a just and equal environment.

5. If you are involved in creating written/web materials to promote your school or organization, do not assume the reader's prior familiarity with the realm [of "college" for example], *period*. When I went to college, I had no idea what a "semester" was, or a "credit". Somehow I sensed that it was not alright to be ignorant of these terms, so I didn't ask anyone. I didn't want to make a fool of myself, after all! Some community colleges in particular have

figured out that the secret language of higher education is not inclusive, and their materials and websites typically provide a glossary of terms.

In the helping professions there is an exclusive language as well, and patients or clients from lower social-class backgrounds are not likely to be familiar with many of those terms. Remember that this is not the result of any cognitive deficiencies on their part; rather, it is a simple lack of exposure to your world. Prepare written materials or introductory videos for the waiting room that explain procedures and policies step by step, assuming no prior knowledge of your elite profession or its associated practices.

6. Tell your story. Rayna Green, who was curator of the Smithsonian Museum's Indian exhibit, spoke at a conference of the National Association for Women Deans, Administrators, and Counselors about a decade ago. She talked about the fact that she is Cherokee, and German, and Jewish. The Cherokee people would prefer that she identify only as Cherokee; the Germans preferred that she identify only as German, and members of the Jewish faith preferred her to claim herself only as a Jew. This, however, felt inauthentic to her. It did not allow her to be the whole person that she is, with the fullness of being all those things. So, she said, "Name your name and claim your home."

Similarly, in an essay entitled "Even if you can't go home again, do it anyway!", Jake Ryan says, "If estrangement and inner conflict are to be resolved, one must go back and embrace the past, even if bonds cannot be fully repaired."[99] If you come from a working-class background yourself, say so. Embrace the fullness of where you come from and all you have learned in your journey through life so far. You are no less than anyone else; in fact, you may be so much more.

By telling your story and saying who you really are, where you really come from, it makes it safe for others to do the same. This is powerful role modeling. When I first said out loud to an audience, "My father was a cook and my mother was a waitress, and neither of them finished high school ..." I was surprised at the lump in my throat, and how my voice shook. What I discovered was that I feared the shaming that goes along with claiming your history. I was also angry about that shaming. I eventually found that my own disclosure made it easier for others to come forward, to claim that part of themselves they had been hiding for fear of rejection and humiliation. These are powerful moments.

7. At the same time, while I encourage you to "Name your name and claim your home," be authentic—if you're not working class, don't claim to be. About a decade ago, I related my story to a new colleague. This young man was clearly struck by what I said, and he replied that he, too, came from a similar background. As time went on in our work together, I happened to find out that his father was a physician, and that his parents owned two homes in a wealthy suburb of a major metropolitan area. They owned two Mercedes as well. He had attended an exclusive private academy. Upon learning this, I felt profoundly betrayed. This was clearly nothing "similar" to my background. I could not understand why this person had tricked me into believing that we shared a common bond. My perspective on it in hindsight is less dramatic, but the lesson remains: be who you are, not who you believe that other person wants or needs you to be.

8. Beware the tendency to see *deficits* only; these individuals have rich cultural attributes and traditions that may be invisible in your particular environment. In a middle-class world, it is easy to define all attributes and behaviors in relation to middle-class standards. As detailed in earlier chapters, individuals from lower social-class backgrounds have been raised with a different set of values. These include speech patterns, behaviors, and defense mechanisms, to name a few. It is possible to carve out space for these characteristics to not be "wrong", but rather to be "different".

    Remember that the things you view as deficits may be exactly the attributes that enabled this person to survive, to move forward, to thrive. A colleague of mine who directed a college program for single parents receiving social services saw this exact pattern playing out. She noted that the students often got themselves in trouble in college by using precisely the same strategies that had enabled them to get this far. As they completed their degree programs and attempted to enter the workforce, again the assertive toughness that had helped them to pull themselves up by their bootstraps was exactly what employers did not want in the workplace. These characteristics did not match the middle-class expectations of gentility in the workplace.[100] However, it is possible to actively value those survival skills, and yet to also value and teach the kinds of characteristics that will be appreciated in the workplace.

    Part of the underlying concept here is to change the image that the culture holds of working-class people. The new image should be a portrait of a person who is as likely as anyone else to be bright, capable, motivated, and hard-working.

9. Avoid "red-neck" jokes, "trailer trash" humor, and slights to country music. While we have thankfully evolved as a society to the point where jokes based on gender, race, religion, and ethnicity are unacceptable (and in some more highly evolved groups, sexual orientation as well), it seems that social class is still a safe topic for humor.

   It is ironic that the recent popularity of the "Blue-Collar Comedy Tour" both on stage and television, stars Jeff Foxworthy, who was previously a manager at IBM corporation, as was his father. This is not exactly what I would call blue collar.

   Those e-mail jokes that circulate endlessly over the Internet may include the "trailer-trash Barbie" genre. You know, push Barbie's belly button and she gets pregnant ... again. Humor like this isn't funny because it assumes the same old things again: poor people are stupid, lazy, and generally haven't a clue. It's OK to make them the subject of ridicule because they won't even realize you're making fun of them.

   Like all humor directed at a single group of people, it is demeaning and reinforces relations of power and subjugation. If you're reading this book, you probably don't need to be dominant. Equality is the goal. Cheap jokes don't get us there.

   Likewise, many people enjoy country music. People who don't care for it (and I am one) reject it on a superficial basis for its soap-opera quality. However, country songs often tell the kinds of real stories that resonate with people from working-class backgrounds. They *are* the coal miners in the songs; they *are* the men getting laid off from work; they *are* the housewives with six children and not enough money for food. They value the songs because they are *real*. The songs represent their experience in our culture, not the middle-class experience that is represented everywhere else in our country—in the media, in the shopping mall, in our government. Even if you don't care for this musical genre, you can learn to respect it for what it represents.

10. Publicly value differences. Truly believing in equality means embracing diversity in many forms. It seems antithetical to the ideal of equality to suggest that some groups are deserving of tolerance, respect, and justice and others are not. When your actions support your beliefs, when you really "walk

the walk", you generate trust. For example, when you publicly confront racist behavior, when you refuse to tolerate sexist jokes, when you stop the harassment of a gay youth, you are demonstrating your dedication to true equality.

If you are the parent of school-age children, encourage your child to invest time in making friends from diverse backgrounds. This is not always easy to do, as some schools are extremely homogeneous, but it is possible. Role model this behavior by creating friendships yourself with diverse adults. If you are unable to do this authentically, take some time to reflect on what the obstacles are within you, and perhaps in your environment, that prevent you from stretching your comfort zone. Are these things you can change?

11. Don't over-generalize. While a great deal of information is presented in this book about persons from working-class backgrounds, and a set of patterns or themes are introduced to suggest general truths about this population, in fact each person is distinctive, each student has a unique personal history, each working-class family has particular tastes, preferences, and habits that may be quite different from what is represented here. Take the time to learn about what makes each individual special, as they no doubt are.

12. Ask them what they need. If you're envisioning yourself as a knight on a white steed swooping in to rescue the impoverished damsel in distress, stop right there. Rather than bestowing your gems upon the needy, ask directly what that person needs in order to overcome the obstacles to their success. The goal might be college, or employment, or advancement. The individual with whom you're working may already know best what s/he needs in order to get there.

A great example of what *not* to do occurs in many towns each year around the holidays. It goes like this: families of means are encouraged to "adopt" a needy family for the holidays. The givers provide food and gifts for people whom they have never met. This is lovely at one level, but problematic at another. There is a bold assumption here that, for example, *I* know what *you* should be eating for this holiday, and what kinds of things your children might need or want. Ask any needy family and they will tell you that they would rather go to a warehouse stocked with donated food and gifts, and choose for *themselves* what works best for their family. Then *they* are selecting what works, they are giving to their children, and providing what they need.

13. Look for ways to change opportunity structures and access to those structures for upward mobility. If you're a college admission officer, for example, what could you do about legacy admissions? What could you do to increase the amount of financial aid available to students with demonstrated financial need? What could you do to make these students feel as if they belonged on campus as much as anyone else?

If you are an employer, what could you do to make sure that employees have access to low-cost day care for their children? In your community, what could you do to promote a living wage? Low-cost health insurance for all?

If you are a school teacher or administrator, what could you do to re-focus the emphasis on learning rather than test scores? There are many opportunities for all of us to educate ourselves about the impact of national legislation regarding education; avail yourself of those opportunities. For example, the August 2005 issue of the journal *Equity and Excellence in Education*[101] focuses on the social justice issues raised by the No Child Left Behind Act. A list of articles provides a glimpse of all there is to be learned beyond the media campaign to support a poorly conceived plan: "No Poor Child Left Un-recruited: How NCLB Codifies and Perpetuates Urban School Militarism," "The Soft Bigotry of Low Expenditures," "No Child Left Behind and the Deliberate Diminishment of Race," "One Hundred Percent Proficiency: A Mission Impossible," "Can Irrational Become Unconstitutional: NCLB's 100% Presuppositions," "Placism in NCLB: How Rural Children Are Left Behind," "When Opting Out is Not a Choice," "A Disability Studies Perspective on the Bush Education Agenda," and "Tension Between the Science of Reading and a Love of Learning." When we educate ourselves about the implications of such legislation, we are better equipped to use our votes for individual action towards justice; and we may choose to lead, or at least participate in, collective action to ensure, in this instance, that indeed no child is left behind. After all, society is socially constructed *by us* and therefore we have the power to reconstruct it in accordance with our vision of a socially just civilization.

Kenneth Oldfield has proposed, in various articles[102], that affirmative hiring policies in higher education which have traditionally included categories of race, gender, sexual orientation, and religion, should also include the socio-economic status of job applicants. Imagine if our colleges, our schools, our hospitals, our mental health clinics, employed professionals who represented *all* of us. This would be a significant step towards embracing diversity and equality in employment practices, with potential positive outcomes for our students, patients, and clients. If you are in a position to influence hiring policies and processes in an organization, perhaps *you* could introduce the idea of including social class origins as an element for consideration to broaden the diversity of your professional staff.

14. Consider the possibility that working-class individuals and families don't need to change; maybe *social institutions* need to change. This includes schools, churches, health care providers, and many others who currently hold a deficit mentality about the poor. Perhaps it is time for our cherished social institutions to actually *be* inclusive, not just *talk* about inclusivity. Maybe, in fact, *society* needs to change significantly in order to achieve our goals of justice and equality.

15. Open the dialog. Begin the discussion. Social class is not, nor should it be, an undiscussable topic. Freire suggested that dialog is the antidote to entrenched ideology; and arguably the best way to fight the culture of silence.[103] Join with others to talk about these issues as they affect your work, your passion for justice, and your personal life. Dialog is not lecturing. The communication must be bi-directional. Dialog is the way to share information, open minds, understand resistance, and hopefully to dislodge complacent ignorance.

16. Brace yourself. In other words, be prepared for controversy if you choose to act. You are ready for change; some will join you with enthusiasm and others will not. You will face possible marginalization and rejection. I once had a vision of what it must be like to be a privileged white male in our culture. In that brief moment, I developed empathy for the men who fight against gender and racial equality. Who would want to give up that comfort and security of being in power, of holding the reins? In fact, many are willing to do so and have gone to great lengths to fight for the kind of equality which will remove them from their sanctuary. Many others will fight to keep what is not rightfully theirs and should be shared by all. You will meet them.

Freire makes the point that the violence of dehumanization that is inflicted upon the oppressed also afflicts the oppressor, though in a different way.[104] Greeting them with respect and empathy will go farther than meeting them with anger and swords. But it will be a battle, nonetheless, and you must be prepared within yourself for that magnificent struggle.

[O]ne of the great paradoxes of education [is] that precisely at the point when you begin to develop a conscience, you must find yourself at war with your society.
—James Baldwin

When I give food to the poor they call me a saint.
When I ask why the poor have no food, they call me a communist.
—Dom Helder Camara

When I dare to be powerful; to use my strength in the service of my vision, then it becomes less and less important whether I am afraid.
—Audre Lorde

Let me say, at the risk of seeming ridiculous, that the true revolutionary is guided by great feelings of love.
—Che Guevara

First they came for the
socialists, and I did not speak out
because I was not a socialist.
Then they came for the trade unionists,
and I did not speak out
because I was not
a trade unionist.
Then they came for the Jews,
and I did not speak out
because I was not a Jew.
Then they came for me,
and there was no one left
to speak for me.
—Pastor Martin Niemoller

A concrete plan of action using current methodology as employed by numerous organizations, including multinational corporations, is included in the following chapter. Appreciative Inquiry is one technique; there are many possibilities. Appreciative Inquiry provides an approach to this difficult subject that allows persons at all social class levels to retain their dignity and humanity, and to work together towards the change that is necessary for social justice.

9

Appreciative Inquiry: A "Best practices" model

From reading this book, you have a good deal of both theoretical and practical information on social class issues and some recommendations for interventions. If you've read this far, you are clearly motivated to make a difference. The goal now is to help others connect their best selves and best practices with class-based knowledge to create environments free of class bias.

One approach which I have found to be effective in working with groups, especially those who might be a bit defensive about their own role in the oppression of working-class individuals, is called Appreciative Inquiry (AI). This approach is based primarily on the work of David Cooperrider and others[105] and is designed for use in organizational development. Fundamentally, AI relies heavily on Kenneth Gergen's work on the social construction of reality. Simply stated, constructionism is a departure from "absolutist" thinking wherein there is only one right answer, one truth. Rather, reality is constructed through social interaction and the truth that I find for myself individually may not be the same as the truth I co-create with you in discussion. Since we live our lives and do our work in relationship with others, the idea that together we create powerful structures of thought and behavior is quite convincing. I certainly encourage you to read more about social constructionism and about Appreciative Inquiry, or attend a workshop on it, before you attempt to employ these methods, as the material presented here represents a simplified view of the full AI spectrum.

Unlike the typical organizational development approach that identifies problems to be solved and mistakes that have been made, in Appreciative Inquiry a positive avenue is employed. The underlying idea is that people are like plants. If you place a plant in a closet with only a crack of light shining through, the plant will naturally lean towards the light. People naturally lean towards learning that affirms them in some way, rather than a lecture on the evils of their thinking and actions.

According to Cooperrider, AI "is about the co-evolutionary search for the best in people, their organizations, and the relevant world around them. In its broadest focus, it involves systematic discovery of what gives 'life' to a living system when it is most alive, most effective, and most constructively capable in economic, ecological, and human terms."[106] The traditional problem-solving model consists of identifying the problem (or problem persons), analyzing the causes of the problems, creating and analyzing possible solutions, and putting a plan in action to remedy the problem. This is familiar to most of us; however, it relies heavily on deficit thinking. The AI model starts with valuing the best of "what is", envisioning "what might be", talking about "what will be", and envisioning "what will be" as if it has already happened.[107] In essence, using AI we ask, "What do we do well in this organization, and how can we do more of that?" "How can we take what works well, and expand it to other areas of our organization that aren't working as well?" We identify our success stories and our talents and skills with the belief that we can apply these in other ways, in other areas. This is clearly a very optimistic view, refreshingly so, and Appreciative Inquiry has enjoyed tremendous success in organizations throughout the world in the past decade or more.

To make these concepts more concrete, I'll use the example of working with a public school staff to describe how this might work. Start and end with inclusivity. It is wonderful to include people at all levels: school administrators, teachers, counselors, aides, cafeteria workers, custodial staff, security, anyone who works there (for wages or as a volunteer). You may have to exert some pressure to get those in power to buy into the idea of inclusivity in this kind of training; this is not how training is usually done. Typically all efforts in traditional training models are focused on top-level administrators, and then there is some hope that learning at the executive level will trickle down to those below and be absorbed as if by osmosis. With AI, it works best to have everyone participate in a very integrated fashion.

The inquiry process might be part of a full-day workshop. The morning would include background information and life stories such as those included in this book. In the afternoon, after explaining what Appreciative Inquiry is, I would move into the process itself. The inquiry process begins with some reflective time. I might say, "Think back through your career in this organization and the class-based encounters you have had. Locate a moment that was a high point, when you felt effective and engaged. Think about how you felt, and what made the situation possible." Give everyone adequate time to bring this memory fully to their mind. Some people may have questions, and since social class has previously been invisible to many people, some may need time to turn this over in their minds and identify an interaction that might indeed have included a class component.

From here we move through a four-part strategy: Interview, Discovery, Dream, and Design. These are explained in greater depth below.

Step I: The Interview

The idea here is to begin sharing our stories in a safe environment. Starting the process with two people talking to each other feels much easier than telling your story to a roomful of listeners. Many people are used to social conversation and need to be instructed in the fine art of interviewing, which is substantially different. An interview is unique in that the interviewer is silent most of the time, and speaks only to begin the conversation with a question, and to elicit depth of detail through active listening and what we call "minimal encouragers."

Active listening, simply stated, requires the listener to be fully present. This includes body language such as facing the speaker, giving him/her eye contact, and quiet attentiveness. The listener's full attention is on the speaker and what s/he is saying. Miminal encouragers are used to convey to the speaker that you are listening and want to hear more. These include nodding the head affirmatively, murmuring "mm-hmm", saying "Tell me more," or asking, "What was that like for you?" These all elicit greater depth of detail, sometimes helping the speaker to recall details that s/he may have forgotten. The goal here is to bring the story to life, in full color, not to get an executive summary.

To start the interview phase, I might say, "Select a partner that you don't know well. Decide which of you will be the interviewer first. Using the following guide (included below), interview your partner for 30 minutes. The interviewer asks the questions and records words, phrases, ideas that are compelling. At the end of 30 minutes, change roles and repeat the interview process." This segment of the process will take an hour altogether. Allowing this amount of time, or more, is important to communicate to the group that each person's story is significant and valued. The guide questions are:

1. Tell me about a time in this organization when you were part of an interaction related to social equality that was exciting, empowering, and energizing. What happened that made it so positive for you? Who was involved? What was the outcome?

2. What is it that you value most about yourself as a person—a friend, colleague, or family member, etc., that was tapped during the experience you described?

3. What do you value about being part of a learning community that promotes social equality?

Here again you can see that we are not pretending to unearth a wholly objective reality which we will then analyze and dissect to find the "problem". We instead personalize interactions and find value in these realities and in the person's discovering them.

In an organization in which only one segment of the possible population of stakeholders is included in this training, you can use this as a train-the-trainer opportunity. The people who go through the full workshop and AI process will go back to their organization and interview others in the organization, then organize groups to share success stories, and move the process forward in this way. For example, it is impractical in a medical setting (such as a hospital) to include everyone at once—who would care for the patients? Workplaces with shift work preclude full attendance as well. In these types of institutions, the domino-effect of interviewing in successive waves, and moving through the rest of the process, is an effective format.

Step II: Discovery

Interest is stimulated in even the most reluctant workshop participant during the discovery phase. Disbelievers begin to see a shimmer of hope. This step of the Appreciative Inquiry process builds on the last step. You will bring together multiple dyads to share each interviewer's notes on the key aspects of the stories shared. Everyone's story and key components are valued, but here we begin to see patterns emerging as stories are compared. Similar themes surface as these new groups work together. Again, the safety of individuals is progressing in small groups. Interviewers share aspects of the stories they heard; pressure is not put on any individual to tell their story. If the interviewers did their job well, each person will feel heard as they listen to the interviewer tell what they gleaned from their narrative. As these key components are shared in small groups, individuals again take notes to record these features.

To make it concrete, my instructions to the group might sound like this: "Now that you've completed your interviews, I'd like you to join with three other dyads so you have eight people altogether. Going around the group, take a few minutes for each person to share the most compelling words, phrases, or ideas they gleaned from interviewing their partner. Take notes as each person shares their insights. Then, identify larger themes or patterns that may have emerged from these reports. As a group, identify the major themes. Select the four or five most compelling themes." (Allow about 60 minutes for this step.)

During the discovery process, the group identifies themes. It's not unusual, if the workshop takes place in a crowded room, for people to overhear other groups discussing the same or very similar themes. This is positive: everyone is right. At the same time, a great variety also emerges in this process, and again, everyone is right. Not all themes will survive the sorting process, however; each small group must decide which themes are most compelling. Depending on the size of the audience with whom you're working, the discovery process may advance from small groups of eight, to groups of 16 before moving into the next phase. In other words, I would have two groups of eight join together and repeat the discovery process, focusing only on the stories and themes they have already identified as the most important to share. This will obviously take more time, so pre-planning on your part is important.

Step III: Dream

The Dream phase builds upon the work done by the groups of eight (and sixteen, if you expand this step). The groups now become creative units as they will use their originality, imagination, and resourcefulness to show other groups their selected themes. For this step, you will want to have flip charts, easels, and colorful markers available.

I might introduce the Dream phase in this way: "In your same group of eight [or 16], create an image of how the organization would function if those major themes were present and fully alive each day. Use drawing or other means of creating this image. Be prepared to share your image and themes with the larger group." (Give the groups at least 30 minutes to complete this segment.)

It is amazing what small groups of people can create in just 30 minutes! I have seen posters, mini-plays, interpretive dance, and various other demonstrations of the themes and patterns which have become vivid in the minds of the group members. Far more important than my reaction is the reaction of the other groups who are privileged to witness these demonstrations when the groups all come together to share their work. And this leads us to the final phase of Appreciative Inquiry, design and delivery.

Step IV: Design and Delivery

To begin this final phase, I would explain to the group, "We will reconvene as a large group to share insights and images. As a group, we'll develop a "provocative proposition"—an affirmative statement that envisions the organization functioning as if all these factors and themes were present daily. Then we'll discuss how to create a design to make the dream reality, and how to deliver the ideal of social equality every day in the life of the organization." (Plan for about 1-2 hours to complete this phase.)

This is a substantial charge for a group who has just learned about social class, oppression, and may be wondering about their ability to change the world, even their small corner of it. However, by this time a significant investment has gone into the process and, though tired, most participants will want to see it through with the expectation of a positive outcome. Many will be energized by the optimistic framing of the AI process, and the stories, ideas, and themes generated by the small groups.

The most important work to be done in this part of the process is the provocative proposition. It is quite a challenge to imagine your possibly dysfunctional, ineffective organization as a high-functioning, effective one that displays all the positive characteristics that you've just been talking about. Let me note here that no two organizations will develop identical desired attributes; the unique character of each organization and the population it serves will shape this outcome. In any case, creating a vision of that desired future may be fraught with anxiety, despite the positive AI frame. Conflicts may arise over which are the best, most important themes to include. Skilled facilitation at this point is critical to the success of the program.

As the vision of the organization emerges, it is important to remind everyone that we are visioning the attributes of the organization *as if* they already existed. So the provocative propositions for a school might include statements like, "We are an organization in which all students achieve at the highest levels, regardless of race or ethnicity." Today, not many (if any) schools in the United States can make such a claim. However, we are writing the propositions *as if* our desired future has already come to pass. There is power is creating such a set of statements, particularly when they are created by a group of people (hopefully everyone at the school) who believe in the themes they have identified from their success stories. It is easy to feel defeated in the face of unequal student achievement, and hard to stand for equality in a meaningful way. AI is one way to focus on the positive, create and articulate a vision for the future, and begin to live that vision *today*.

Obviously, it is not enough to envision a desired future but not plan for making that vision a reality. The detailed work of designing a plan for action may take some time, and probably won't fit into a day-long workshop format (though you might begin it there). The leadership of the organization needs to take over at this point, and make space in the life of the organization to enable all stakeholders to begin planning for change. This is a complex task, and the process will be unique to each organization based on all those characteristics previously mentioned, as well as the requirements of the vision they have co-created.

Appreciative Inquiry refuses to dwell on the actual losses or perceived failures of the past; rather, the focus is on our successes and how we can make those an expanded part of the future of an organization. AI is not about deficits, but about attributes and characteristics of people and organizations that enable us to create the future we want. When we are talking about social class issues, and the long history of injustice and inequality in our society, perhaps it is time to look at our best practices and envision how we can expand that vision of equality and justice in our organizations and in our society, beginning now.

10

Conclusion: It's just the beginning...

This is the end of the book, but it's just the beginning of the story. Remember, *you* can make a difference! Look at where you've been; look at where you're going. Where will *you* begin to change the world? Like choosing a charity to support, finding a way to create space for another person's opportunity and achievement is a personal choice. It can also be a frightening idea due to the sheer magnitude of the challenge. Don't let that discourage you. The only sure way to fail is to put this book away and think that maybe next week you'll do something to create change ... and when you're too busy next week, you put it off until the following week. And somehow, the anointed day for initiating action never comes. This is how we get stuck with the master-servant duality.

Some people think of lower social-class existence as a curse, a miserable existence, or a failure. If that is your conclusion upon reading this book, then I have neglected to share the positive side of the story with you. Many of us from lower social-class backgrounds revel in the values we learned and continue to embrace. We value our families, our communities, and our histories. We see the deficits in the people and places in our lives, but we don't always focus on them. Those of us whose stories are included in this book celebrate our own good fortune in escaping poverty and temper that with the knowledge of our hard work and sacrifices to do just that. Some of us labor under a mountain of student loan debt, but that is still better than never having attempted to do that of which we knew we were capable. We mourn the loss of friends and family who could not bear to see us turn into "the other" as we moved up socioeconomically and moved into careers that are incomprehensible, and yet we understand their choice. We don't fit in, and we can't turn back, but we have made a choice to create a better future; not just for ourselves, not just for our families, but for our world. Within the pain of loss and isolation there is still room for optimism and satisfaction. As you'll find, sometimes joy and laughter emerge from the strangest places.

Our town had no dentist. There were undoubtedly plenty of bad teeth to keep a dental professional busy, but any dentist looking at the community would not see the possibility of a lucrative practice. So, we drove to the next town. Our dentist seemed ancient. So did his equipment. But, we had no dental insurance, so this was the best we could do. I can recall the drill accidentally hitting my tongue on several occasions, and actively resisted going, delaying visits such that there were frequently years in between. I had a permanent molar removed at age 12 due to decay, and nothing to prevent the adjacent teeth from leaning into that space, creating more dental problems.

At the inevitable point in early adolescence when braces were recommended for my crooked tooth (just one, right in front), a few of my friends already had braces and I had heard both the horror stories of physical pain and what seemed like an exorbitant cost for such pain. My dentist recommended braces for me, and outlined the procedure and price. My parents haltingly asked me if I would like to get the braces. The unconscious looks of concern on their faces reflected their inner struggle regarding a cost they could ill afford. It only took me a moment to answer, No, I don't want them.

Inside, I resolved to smile less so that my offensive crooked tooth would not be seen, nor my numerous silver fillings. I was quite successful in this, so much so that I held back smiles for nearly two decades. People who really knew me and cared, mentioned this, because often the effort of keeping my lips over my teeth made my smiles look like a grimace or cat-who-swallowed-the-canary leer. It wasn't until I had good dental insurance of my own that I got my bad teeth capped or repaired with less visible fillings and learned to accept the crooked one as part of my personality—a sign of character, as one of my friends called it. Then the clenched lips relaxed and the lost smiles of childhood slowly returned. I had to learn how to smile naturally all over again. My big gold crowns flash when I smile broadly and throw my head back in a big laugh. That's my jewelry.

So, smile. Let your good teeth—or bad teeth—show. It doesn't matter today whether you're servant or master; what matters is what you do with the knowledge you have in the service of justice and equality.

Will you change the world? Will you be that one person who makes a difference?

Epilogue

A future book on social class issues is in the planning and research stages as of this writing. If you're from a working-class or poverty-class background and you'd like to contribute your story, please contact me. I will be seeking information about people's lives that address these kinds of questions:

What motivated you to continue in your education or towards a professional career? What obstacles did you encounter? Was there a special person(s) who encouraged you?

What kinds of experiences did you have with "helping professionals" (counselors, doctors, nurses, human services workers, and others) that suggested to you that you were being treated differently based on your social class background?

How do you think your social class background has influenced your choice of friends and/or romantic partners? Did it make a difference to you, or to them? Are there specific instances you can point to when your social class background(s) created points of conflict or cohesion?

How do you define success? What has contributed to making you successful today, in your career, relationships, or other areas of your life?

To send your stories to me, please be sure to put "Homemade" in the subject line and send it to me at: signe_m_kastberg@post.harvard.edu. Include your email address and your postal mailing address. I will then send you some permission forms that would give me your approval to share your story in my next book. I look forward to reading your story!

Endnotes

Introduction

1 All names used are pseudonyms. Quotes are from interviews conducted in February 1997 and May 1997, unless otherwise specified.

Chapter 1

2 Paulo Freire, 1970. *Cultural Action for Freedom*. Cambridge: Harvard Educational Review.

3 Janny Scott and David Leonhardt, "Class in America: Shadowy Lines That Still Divide" *New York Times* May 15, 2005.

4 Pierre Bourdieu and Jean-Claude Passeron, *Reproduction in Education, Society, and Culture*. Translated from the French by Richard Nice. London: Sage Publications. Pp. xi.

5 Barbara J. Peters. 1998. *The Head Start Mother: Low-Income Mothers' Empowerment through Participation*. Taylor & Francis.

6 Pseudonym, e-mail message to working-class academics listserv with permission to use sent to author, March 9, 2005.

7 Jamie Johnson, *Born Rich*. October 2004.

Chapter 2

8 *The International Encyclopedia of Sociology*, edited by Michael Mann.1984. Continuum Publishing Co., p. 45.

9 Paul Fussell, 1983. *Class: A guide through the American status system*. New York: Simon & Schuster.

10 *The International Encyclopedia of Sociology*, edited by Michael Mann.1984. Continuum Publishing Co., p. 45.

11 Janny Scott and David Leonhardt, "Class in America: Shadowy Lines That Still Divide" *New York Times* May 15, 2005.

12 Ibid.

13 McDermott, J. 1969 Overclass/underclass: Knowledge is power. *The Nation*, 208, 458-462.

14 Janny Scott and David Leonhardt, "Class in America: Shadowy Lines That Still Divide" *New York Times* May 15, 2005.
15 Beeghley, L. *The structure of social stratification in the United States.*1989. Boston, MA: Allyn and Bacon.

Chapter 3

16 Judith Touchton and Lynne Davis 1991. *Fact book on women in higher education.* New York: Macmillan Publishing Company.
17 C&EN Special Report: 2001 Salary Survey. Nov. 19, 2001, Vol. 79, NO. 47, CESNEAR 79 47 pp. 71-73. ISSN 0009-2347. Retrieved January 11, 2005. http://pubs.acs.org/cen/topstory/7947/7947sci2.html#Anchor-10943.
18 Nakao, K. and Treas, J. 1990 Computing 1989 occupational prestige scores. General social survey methodological report No. 70. National Opinion Research Center.
Nakao, K. and Treas, J. 1992 The 1989 socioeconomic index of occupations: Construction from the 1989 occupational prestige scores. General social survey methodological report No. 74. National Opinion Research Center.
Nakao, K., Hodge, R. and Treas, J. 1990 On revising prestige scores for all occupations. General social survey methodological report No. 69. National Opinion Research Center.
19 Source: Nakao, K. and Treas, J. 1990 Computing 1989 occupational prestige scores. General social survey methodological report No. 70. National Opinion Research Center.
20 Ibid.
21 Touchton and Davis, 1991.
22 http://www.postsecondary.org/archives/Excel/Educational%20 Attainment%20by%20State_pw_protected.xls.
23 Ibid.
24 http://www.wa.gov/research/issues/documents/2004-05TuitionandFeeRates-ANationalComparisonJanuary2005.pdf
25 Ibid
26 Michael McPherson and Morton Schapior, 1998 *The Studend Aid Game: Meeting Need and Rewarding Talent in American Higher Education.* Princeton: Princeton University Press. Pp. 143.
27 "Family Income and Higher Education Opportunity 1970 to 2003." *Postsecondary Education Opportunity*, Number 156, June 2005.

28 Birenbaum, W. 1986. From mass to class in higher education. In L.S. Zwerling, ed. The community college and its critics. *New Directions for Community Colleges*, A.M. Cohen and F.B. Brawer, Eds., 54, 3-12.

29 O'Barr, J. 1986. Re-entry women in the academy: The contributions of a feminist perspective. In C. Pearson, D. Shavlik, and J. Touchton, eds., *Educating the majority: Women challenge tradition in higher education* (pp. 90-101). New York: Macmillan Publishing Co.

30 Cited in London, H. 1986. Strangers to our shores. In L.S. Zwerling, ed. The community college and its critics. *New Directions for Community Colleges*, A.M. Cohen and F.B. Brawer, Eds., 54, 91-100.

31 Ibid, 98.

32 London, H. 1992 Transformations: Cultural challenges faced by first-generation students. In L.S. Zwerling and H. London, eds. First-generation students: Confronting the cultural issues. *New Directions for Community Colleges*, A.M. Cohen and F.B. Brawer, Eds., 80, 5.

33 Mortenson, T. 1995. Educational attainment by family income 1970 to 1994. *Postsecondary Education Opportunity*, 41, 14.

Chapter 4

34 Interview with university faculty/administrator, May 5, 1997.

35 Pseudonym, e-mail message to working-class academics listserv with permission to use sent to author, March 21, 2001.

36 Gary W. Evans, 2004. The Environment of Childhood Poverty. *American Psychologist* 59 (2), 77-92; p. 77.

37 Quay, L.C. and Jarrett, O.S. 1986. Teachers' interactions with middle and lower SES preschool boys and girls. *Journal of Educational Psychology*, 78, 495-498.

38 Belenky, M., Clinchy, B., Goldberger, N., and Tarule, J. 1986. *Women's ways of knowing: The development of self, voice, and mind.* Basic Books.

39 Oakes, J. 1985. *Keeping track: How schools structure inequality.* New Haven, CT: Yale University Press.

40 Pseudonym, e-mail message to working-class academics listserv with permission to use sent to author, October 26, 2001.

41 McCall, G.J. and Simmons, J.L. 1982. *Social psychology: A sociological approach.* New York: The Free Press.

42 Interview with university faculty/administrator, March 5, 1997.

43 Ruby Payne. 1998. *A Framework for Understanding Poverty.* Highlands, TX: RFT Publishing Co.

44 Interview with higher education faculty/administrator, February 26, 1997.

45 McCall and Simmons, 1982, *Social Psychology.*

46 Cole, J. 1996. Beyond Prejudice [on line]. Available: www.eburg.comm/ beyond.prejudice, as cited in P. Sharma and D. Lucero-Miller. 1998. Beyond political correctness. In T. Singelis [Ed.] *Teaching about culture, ethnicity, and diversity.* Sage Publications: Thousand Oaks CA. pp. 191-196.

47 Brantlinger, E. 1993. *The politics of social class in secondary school.* New York: Teachers College Press.

48 Pipher, M. 1994. *Reviving Ophelia: Saving the selves of adolescent girls.* New York: Ballantine Books.

49 Victor Lavy and Analía Schlosser May 2007, "Mechanisms and Impacts of Gender Peer Effects at School. http://www.iza.org/conference_files/TAM2007/ schlosser_a1994.pdf, retrieved September 7, 2007.

50 Denmark, F. L. and Paludi, M., Eds. 1993. *Psychology of women: A handbook of issues and theories.* Westport, CT: Greenwood Press.

51 Matlin, M. 1993. *The psychology of women.* Fort Worth, TX: Harcourt Brace Jovanovich.

52 Ibid.

53 Oakes, *Keeping Track;* and Brantlinger, *The Politics of Social Class.*

54 Pipher, *Reviving Ophelia.*

55 Ibid.

56 Sandler, B., Silverberg, L., and Hall, R. 1996. *The chilly classroom climate: A guide to improve the education of women.* Washington, DC: The National Association for Women in Education.

57 Ibid.

58 Hart, D., Maloney, J. and Damon, W. 1987. The meaning and development of identity. In Honess, T. and Yardley, K. (eds.). *Self and identity: Perspectives across the lifespan* (pp. 121-133). London: Routledge and Kegan Paul.

59 Brantlinger, *The politics of social class.*

60 Oakes, *Keeping Track.*

61 Brantlinger, *The politics of social class.*

62 Pseudonym, e-mail message to working-class academics listserv with permission to use sent to author, June 25, 1999.

63 Interview with university faculty/administrator, May 7, 1997.

64 Evans, M. 1995. Culture and class. In Blair, M., Holland, J., and Sheldon, S. (eds.). *Identity and diversity: Gender and the experience of education* (pp. 61-73). Clevedon, UK: Multilingual Matters Ltd.

65 Dannefer, D. 1992. On the conceptualization of context in developmental discourse: Four meanings of context and their implications. In Featherman, D., Lerner, R. and Perlmutter, M. (eds.). *Life-span development and behavior* (pp. 83-110). Hillsdale, NJ: Lawrence Erlbaum Associates.

66 Brantlinger, *The politics of social class.*

67 Ibid.

68 Ibid.

69 Ibid, 119.

70 Ibid, 119.

71 Ibid, 133.

72 Emmett, A. 1996. *Our sisters' promised land: Women, politics, and Israeli-Palestinian coexistence.* Ann Arbor, MI: The University of Michigan Press. Matlin, M. 1993. *The psychology of women.* Fort Worth, TX: Harcourt Brace Jovanovich.

73 Interview with university faculty/administrator, May 6, 1997.

74 Bidwell, C. and Friedkin, N. 1988. The sociology of education. In N. Smelser, (ed.) *Handbook of sociology,* Newbury Park, CA: Sage Publications.

75 Brantlinger, 176.

76 Ibid, 177.

77 Bidwell and Friedkin, *Handbook of sociology.*

78 Dannefer, D. and Perlmutter, M. 1990. Development as a multidimensional process: Individual and social constituents. *Human Development, 33,* 108-137.

79 Miller, D. and Kastberg, S. 1995. Of blue collars and ivory towers: Women from blue-collar backgrounds in higher education. *Roeper Review, 18,* 27-33.

80 Rosenbaum, J. 1978. *The structure of opportunity in school.* Social Forces, 57, 236-256.

81 Brantlinger, *The politics of social class* and Miller and Kastberg, Of Blue Collars and Ivory Towers.

82 Brantlinger, 178.

83 Pseudonym, e-mail message to working-class academics listserv with permission to use sent to author, March 23, 2001.

84 Interview with university faculty/administrator, May 7, 1997.

85 Focus group interview with university faculty/administrator, February 26, 1997.

86 Focus group interview with university faculty/administrator, February 26, 1997.

87 Interview with higher education faculty/administrator, April 30, 1997.

88 Interview with higher education faculty/administrator, May 1, 1997.

Chapter 5

89 Pierre Bourdieu and Jean-Claude Passeron, *Reproduction in Education, Society, and Culture*. Translated from the French by Richard Nice. London: Sage Publications, pp. 255.

Chapter 7

90 Pierre Bourdieu, *Distinction: A social critique of the judgement of taste*. Translated by Richard Nice. 1984. Cambridge: Harvard University Press. Pp. 107-108.

91 Unless otherwise noted, all direct quotes in this chapter are the result of interviews conducted in a group format on February 26, 1997, or individual interviews conducted with various faculty/administrators in higher education in May, 1997.

92 Clance, P.R. 1985. *The impostor phenomenon*. Atlanta: Peachtree Press.

93 Ibid, 5.

94 Ibid.

95 Pseudonym, e-mail message to working-class academics listserv with permission to use sent to author, November 2, 2001.

96 Al Lubrano, 2004. *Limbo: Blue-collar roots, white-collar dreams*. Hoboken: John Wiley & Sons, Inc.

Chapter 8

97 Freire, Paulo. 1970. *Cultural Action for Freedom*. Cambridge: Center for the Study of Development and Social Change. Pp. 27.

98 K. Patricia Cross, 1971. *Beyond the Open Door: New students to higher education*. San Francisco: Jossey-Bass.

99 Ryan, Jake, 1996. "Even if you can't go home again, do it anyway!" *Race, Gender & Class*. Vol. 4, No. 1, 1996 (83-102). pp. 101.

100 Nancy Boldt, Personal communication, 1992.

101 Gerald W. Bracey, ed. August 2005. *Equity and Excellence in Education*, Volume 35 #3. Taylor and Francis.

102 Oldfield, Kenneth. "Expanding Economic Democracy in American Higher Education: A two-step approach to hiring more teachers from poverty—and working-class backgrounds" in *Journal of Higher Education Policy and Management*, Vol. 29, No. 2, July 2007, pp. 217-230. See also "How Can We Democratize Higher Education of We Don't Count the Votes? A Master of Public

Administration Case Study" in *Journal of Public Affairs Education*, Vol 13, No. 1, Winter 2007, pp. 133-146.
103 Freire, Paulo. 1970. *Cultural Action for Freedom*. Cambridge: Center for the Study of Development and Social Change. Pp. vii.
104 Freire, P. 2004. *Pedagogy of the Oppressed*. New York: Continuum. Pp. 44.

Chapter 9

105 David L. Cooperrider, Peter Sorensen, Therese Yaeger, and Diana Whitney, Eds. 2001. *Appreciative Inquiry: An emerging direction for organization development*. Champaign, IL: Stipes Publishing LLC.
106 Ibid, p. 7.
107 Ibid, p. 25.

About the Author

Signe M. Kastberg is Associate Professor and Director of the M.S. Program in Mental Health Counseling at St. John Fisher College in Rochester, New York. She earned an A.A.S. degree from the State University of New York at Cobleskill, and a B.A. from Skidmore College. She completed a Master's degree in Education at Harvard University, and was subsequently awarded a Fulbright scholarship for independent research in Denmark. Upon returning to the United States, she worked in higher education as a Director of Continuing Education for a number of colleges and universities, and in private business. She completed a Ph.D. in Human Development at the University of Rochester and a Graduate Certificate in Gender and Women's Studies. During her doctoral studies, she was designated as a Scandling Scholar, May Eddy Butler Walker Scholar, and Jack K. Miller Memorial Scholar. The National Association for Women in Education recognized Dr. Kastberg's dissertation research with the Ruth Strang Research Award.

Upon completion of her doctoral degree, Dr. Kastberg served as Assistant Professor of Counseling and Human Development at the University of Rochester and subsequently held a joint appointment as Assistant Professor of Counselor Education and college counselor at SUNY Brockport. She has served as a counselor at Cornell University and as Assistant Professor at Ithaca College. She is a

National Certified Counselor (NCC) and a licensed mental health counselor (LMHC) in New York State.

Dr. Kastberg's research interests focus on the intersection of social class with gender, education, and mental health services. She has been a frequent presenter on the ways in which talented girls and women from lower social-class backgrounds are discouraged from upward career and social mobility; and particularly the ways in which counselors participate in this process of social reproduction. Dr. Kastberg is also a qualified administrator and interpreter of the Myers-Briggs Type Indicator (MBTI), and enjoys working with a variety of groups in demonstrating how an understanding of personality types can enhance relationships at work, home, and in educational environments. Stress management and mood enhancement through African drumming is a current interest.

Bibliography

Aboud, F. and Ruble, D. (1987). Identity constancy in children: Developmental processes and implications. In Honess, T. and Yardley, K. (eds.). *Self and identity: Perspectives across the lifespan* (pp. 95-107). London: Routledge and Kegan Paul.

Acker, J. (1973). Women and social stratification: A case of intellectual sexism. *American Journal of Sociology,* 78 (4), 174-183.

Anderson, B. (1991). *Imagined communities: Reflections on the origin and spread of nationalism.* London: Verso.

Astin, H., Astin, A., Bisconti, A., and Frankel, H. (1972). *Higher education and the disadvantaged student.* Washington, DC: Human Service Press.

Bateson, M.C. (1990). *Composing a life.* New York: Penguin Group.

Beeghley, L. (1989). *The structure of social stratification in the United States.* Boston, MA: Allyn and Bacon.

Belenky, M., Clinchy, B., Goldberger, N., and Tarule, J. (1986). *Women's ways of knowing: The development of self, voice, and mind.* Basic Books.

Bidwell, C. and Friedkin, N. (1988). The sociology of education. In N. Smelser, (ed.) *Handbook of sociology,* Newbury Park, CA: Sage Publications.

Birenbaum, W. (1986). From mass to class in higher education. In L.S. Zwerling, ed. *The community college and its critics.* New Directions for Community Colleges, A.M. Cohen and F.B. Brawer, Eds., 54, 3-12.

Blair, M., Holland, J., and Sheldon, S. (1993). *Identity and diversity: Gender and the experience of education.* Clevedon, UK: Multilingual Matters Ltd.

Blascovich, J. and Tomaka, J. (1991). Measures of self-esteem. In J. Robinson, P. Shaver and L. Wrightsman (Eds.), *Measures of personality and social psychological attitudes*. 1. (pp. 115-160). San Diego, CA: Academic Press Inc.

Blumer, H. (1969). *Symbolic interactionism: Perspective and method*. Englewood Cliffs, NJ: Prentice-Hall, Inc.

Bott, E. (1957). *Family and social network: Roles, norms, and external relationships in ordinary urban families*. London, England: Tavistock Publishers.

Bourdieu, P. 1984. *Distinction: A social critique of the judgement of taste*. Translated by Richard Nice. Cambridge: Harvard University Press.

Bourdieu, P. (1977). *Outline of a theory of practice*. Cambridge, UK: Cambridge University Press.

Bourdieu, P. and Passeron, J.C. (1990). *Reproduction in education, society, and culture*. London: Sage.

Brantlinger, E. (1993). *The politics of social class in secondary school*. New York: Teachers College Press.

Bronfenbrenner, U. (1989). Ecological systems theory. *Annals of Child Development*, 6, 187-249.

Bruck, M. and Tucker, G.R. (1974). Social class differences in the acquisition of school language. *Merrill-Palmer Quarterly*, 20, 205-220.

C&EN Special Report: 2001 Salary Survey. Nov. 19, 2001, Vol. 79, NO. 47, CESNEAR 79 47 pp. 71-73. ISSN 0009-2347. Retrieved January 11, 2005. http://pubs.acs.org/cen/topstory/7947/7947sci2.html#Anchor-10943.

Clance, P.R. (1985). *The impostor phenomenon*. Atlanta: Peachtree Press.

Clandinin, D.J., and Connelly, F.M. (1994). Personal experience methods. In Denzin, N. and Lincoln, Y., Eds.. *Handbook of qualitative research* (pp. 413-427). Thousand Oaks, CA: Sage Publications.

Clark, S. and Corcoran, M. (1986). Perspectives on the professional socialization of women faculty: A case of accumulative disadvantage? *Journal of Higher Education*, 57, 20-43.

Cole, J. 1996. *Beyond Prejudice [on line]*. Available: www.eburg.comm/ beyond.prejudice, as cited in P. Sharma and D. Lucero-Miller. 1998. Beyond political correctness. In T. Singelis [Ed.] *Teaching about culture, ethnicity, and diversity*. Sage Publications: Thousand Oaks CA. pp. 191-196.

Cookson Jr., P.W. and Persell, C.H (1985). *Preparing for power: America's elite boarding schools*. Basic Books.

Cooperrider, D., Sorensen, P., Yaeger, T, and Whitney, D., Eds. (2001). *Appreciative Inquiry: An emerging direction for organization development*. Champaign, IL: Stipes Publishing LLC.

Crane, D.M. (1969). Social class origin and academic success: The influence of two stratification systems on academic careers. *Sociology of Education*, 42, 1-17.

Dannefer, D. (1992). On the conceptualization of context in developmental discourse: Four meanings of context and their implications. In Featherman, D., Lerner, R. and Perlmutter, M. (eds.). *Life-span development and behavior* (pp. 83-110). Hillsdale, NJ: Lawrence Erlbaum Associates.

Dannefer, D. and Perlmutter, M. (1990). Development as a multidimensional process: Individual and social constituents. *Human Development*, 33, 108-137.

de Toqueville, A. (1900). *Democracy in America*. New York: P.F. Collier & Son.

Denmark, F. L. and Paludi, M., Eds. (1993). *Psychology of women: A handbook of issues and theories*. Westport, CT: Greenwood Press.

Denzin, N. and Lincoln, Y., Eds. (1994). *Handbook of qualitative research*. Thousand Oaks, CA: Sage Publications.

Dews, C.L., and Law, C.L., Eds. (1995). *This fine place so far from home*. Philadelphia: Temple University Press.

Doyle, A., Ceschin, F., Tessier, O, and Doehring, P. (1991). The relation of age and social class factors in children's social pretend play to cognitive and symbolic activity. *International Journal of Behavioral Development*, 14 (4), 395-410.

Eisler, R. (1987). *The chalice and the blade*. New York: Harper and Row.

Emmett, A. (1996). *Our sisters' promised land: Women, politics, and Israeli-Palestinian coexistence*. Ann Arbor, MI: The University of Michigan Press.

Epstein, C. F. (1973). Positive effects of the multiple negative: Explaining the success of black professional women. *American Journal of Sociology*, 78, 912-935.

Epstein, C.F. (1981). Women in sociological analysis: New scholarship versus old paradigms. *Soundings*, 64 (4), 485-498.

Erikson, E. (1968). *Identity: Youth and crisis*. New York: Norton.

Evans, G.W. (2004). The Environment of Childhood Poverty. *American Psychologist* 59 (2), 77-92.

Evans, M. (1995). Culture and class. In Blair, M., Holland, J., and Sheldon, S. (eds.). *Identity and diversity: Gender and the experience of education* (pp. 61-73). Clevedon, UK: Multilingual Matters Ltd.

Fannin, P. (1979). The relation between ego-identity status and sex-role attitude, work-role salience, atypicality of major, and self-esteem in college women. *Journal of Vocational Behavior*, 14, 12-22.

Feagans, L. and Fendt, K. (1991). The effects of intervention and social class on children's answers to concrete and abstract questions. *Journal of Applied Developmental Psychology*, 12, 115-130.

Fine, M. (1994). Working the hyphens: Reinventing self and other in qualitative research. In Denzin, N. and Lincoln, Y., Eds.. *Handbook of qualitative research* (pp. 70-82). Thousand Oaks, CA: Sage Publications.

Fontana, A., and Frey, J. (1994). Interview: The art of science. In Denzin, N. and Lincoln, Y., Eds.. *Handbook of qualitative research* (pp. 361-376). Thousand Oaks, CA: Sage Publications.

Frankl, V. (1992). *Man's search for meaning*, 4th ed. Boston: Beacon Press.

Freire, P. (1970). *Cultural Action for Freedom.* Cambridge: Center for the Study of Development and Social Change.

Freire, P. (2004). *Pedagogy of the Oppressed.* New York: Continuum.

Geertz, C. (1973). *The interpretation of cultures.* New York: Basic Books.

Gekas, V. and Mortimer, J. (1987). Stability and change in the self-concept from adolescence to adulthood. In Honess, T. and Yardley, K. (eds.). *Self and identity: Perspectives across the lifespan* (pp. 265-286). London: Routledge and Kegan Paul.

Gilligan, C. (1982). *In a different voice.* Cambridge, MA: Harvard University Press.

Gittell, M. (1986). A place for women? In L.S. Zwerling, ed. *The community college and its critics.* New Directions for Community Colleges, A.M. Cohen and F.B. Brawer, Eds., 54, 71-80.

Grossman, H. and Grossman S. (1994). *Gender issues in education.* Boston, MA: Allyn and Bacon.

Guba, E., and Lincoln, Y. (1994). Competing paradigms in qualitative research. In Denzin, N. and Lincoln, Y., Eds. *Handbook of qualitative research* (pp. 105-117). Thousand Oaks, CA: Sage Publications.

Gubrium, J., Holstein, J., and Buckholdt, D. (1994). *Constructing the life course.* Dix Hill, New York: General Hall, Inc. Publishers.

Hall, R. and Sandler, B. (1982). *The classroom climate: A chilly one for women?* Washington, DC: Project on the Status and Education of Women; Association of American Colleges.

Harre, R. (1987). The social construction of selves. In Yardley, K. and Honess, T., (eds.). *Self and identity: Psychosocial perspectives* (pp. 41-52). Chichester, UK: John Wiley and Sons.

Hart, D., Maloney, J. and Damon, W. (1987). The meaning and development of identity. In Honess, T. and Yardley, K. (eds.). *Self and identity: Perspectives across the lifespan* (pp. 121-133). London: Routledge and Kegan Paul.

Hollingshead, A. and F. Redlich (1958). *Social class and mental illness.* New York: Wiley.

Honess, T. and Yardley, K., Eds. (1987). *Self and identity: Perspectives across the lifespan.* London: Routledge and Kegan Paul.

Honess, T. and Yardley, K., Eds. (1987). Self and social structure: An introductory review. In Yardley, K. and Honess, T., (eds.). *Self and identity: Psychosocial perspectives* (pp. 83-88). Chichester, UK: John Wiley and Sons.

hooks, b. (1990). *Yearning: Race, gender, and cultural politics.* Boston: South End Press.

Jacklin, C.N. (1989). Female and male: Issues of gender. *American Psychologist,* 44, 127-133.

Jordan, J. (1991). The relational self: A new perspective for understanding women's development. In Strauss, J. and Goethals, G., (eds.). *The self: Interdisciplinary approaches* (pp. 136-149). New York: Springer-Verlag.

Kanter, R.M. (1977). *Men and women of the corporation.* New York: Basic Books.

Karabel, J. (1986). Community colleges and social stratification in the 1980's. In L.S. Zwerling, ed. *The community college and its critics.* New Directions for Community Colleges, A.M. Cohen and F.B. Brawer, Eds., 54, 13-30.

Kasl, S. (1967). Status inconsistency: Some conceptual and methodological considerations. In J. Robinson, R. Athanasious, and K. Head, (Eds.), *Measures of occupational attitudes and occupational characteristics* (pp. 377-390). Survey Research Center, Institute for Social Research.

Kastberg, S., and Miller, D. (1996). Of blue collars and ivory towers: Women from blue-collar backgrounds in higher education. In K. Arnold, K. Noble, and R. Subotnik (eds.) *Remarkable women: Perspectives on female talent development,* (pp. 49-68). Cresskill, NJ: Hampton Press, Inc.

Keller, E. F. (1985). *Reflections on gender and science.* New Haven, CT: Yale University Press.

Kleinberg, S. (1979) Success and the working class. *Journal of American Culture,* 2, 123-138.

Kohn, M.L. (1969) *Class and conformity: A study in values.* Homewood, IL: The Dorsey Press.

Laing, R.D. (1967) *The politics of experience.* New York: Pantheon Books.

Lehtinen, V. and Joukamaa, M. (1994). Epidemiology of depression: Prevalence, risk factors and treatment situation. *Acta Psychiatra Scandinavia,* Supplement 377: 7-10.

Levi-Strauss, C. (1966). *The savage mind.* (trans.) Chicago: University of Chicago Press.

Lipset, S.M. and Ladd Jr., E.C. (1979). The changing social origins of American academics. In R.K. Merton, J.S. Coleman and P.H. Rossi (Eds.), *Qualitative and quantitative social research: Papers in honor of Paul F. Lazarsfeld* (pp. 319-338). New York: The Free Press.

London, H. (1986). Strangers to our shores. In L.S. Zwerling, ed. *The community college and its critics.* New Directions for Community Colleges, A.M. Cohen and F.B. Brawer, Eds., 54, 91-100.

London, H. (1992). Transformations: Cultural challenges faced by first-generation students. In L.S. Zwerling and H. London, eds. *First-generation students: Confronting the cultural issues.* New Directions for Community Colleges, A.M. Cohen and F.B. Brawer, Eds., 80, 5-12.

Luzzo, D. (1992). Ethnic group and social class differences in college students' career development. *Career Development Quarterly,* 41, 161-173.

Maccoby, E.E. and Jacklin, C.N. (1974). *The psychology of sex differences.* Stanford: Stanford University Press.

Malinowski, B. (1922, 1961, 1984). *Argonauts of the western Pacific.* Prospect Heights, IL: Waveland Press, Inc.

Malor, U. (1995). Migration and education. In Blair, M., Holland, J., and Sheldon, S. (eds.). *Identity and diversity: Gender and the experience of education* (pp. 39-50). Clevedon, UK: Multilingual Matters Ltd.

Marino, T. (1995). Isolation, lack of role models blamed for low career expectations in rural areas. *Counseling Today*, 38, 1-12.

Martinez Thorne, Y. (1995). Achievement motivation in high achieving Latina women. *Roeper Review*, 18, 44-49.

Matlin, M. (1993). *The psychology of women*. Fort Worth, TX: Harcourt Brace Jovanovich.

May, R. (1953). *Man's search for himself.* New York: Delta Books.

McCall, G.J. and Simmons, J.L. (1982). *Social psychology: A sociological approach*. New York: The Free Press.

McDermott, J. (1969). Overclass/underclass: Knowledge is power. *The Nation*, 208, 458-462.

Mecca, A., Smelser, N., and Vasconcellos, J., eds. (1989). *The social importance of self esteem*. Berkeley, CA: University of California Press.

Miller, D. and Kastberg, S. (1995). Of blue collars and ivory towers: Women from blue-collar backgrounds in higher education. *Roeper Review*, 18, 27-33.

Miller, J. (1976). *Toward a new psychology of women*. Boston, MA: Beacon Press.

Mortenson, T. (1995). Educational attainment by family income 1970 to 1994. *Postsecondary Education Opportunity*, 41, 1-8.

Mortenson, T. (1995). Think about this for a while…. *Postsecondary Education Opportunity*, 41, 14.

Mortenson, T. (1995). Parental educational attainment and chance for college. *Postsecondary Education Opportunity*, 33, 1-8.

Nakao, K. and Treas, J. (1990). Computing 1989 occupational prestige scores. General social survey methodological report No. 70. National Opinion Research Center.

Nakao, K. and Treas, J. (1992). The 1989 socioeconomic index of occupations: Construction from the 1989 occupational prestige scores. General social survey methodological report No. 74. National Opinion Research Center.

Nakao, K., Hodge, R. and Treas, J. (1990). On revising prestige scores for all occupations. General social survey methodological report No. 69. National Opinion Research Center.

Oakes, J. (1985). *Keeping track: How schools structure inequality.* New Haven, CT: Yale University Press.

O'Barr, J. (1986). Re-entry women in the academy: The contributions of a feminist perspective. In C. Pearson, D. Shavlik, and J. Touchton, eds., *Educating the majority: Women challenge tradition in higher education (pp. 90-101).* New York: Macmillan Publishing Co.

Olesen, V. (1994). Feminisms and models of qualitative research. In Denzin, N. and Lincoln, Y., Eds.. *Handbook of qualitative research* (pp. 158-174). Thousand Oaks, CA: Sage Publications.

Perry Jr., W.G. (1970). *Forms of intellectual and ethical development in the college years.* New York: Holt, Rinehart and Winston, Inc.

Peters, Barbara. 1998. *The Head Start Mother: Low-income mothers' empowerment through participation.* New York: Garland Publishing Inc.

Pipher, M. (1994). *Reviving Ophelia: Saving the selves of adolescent girls.* New York: Ballantine Books.

Quay, L.C. and Jarrett, O.S. (1986). Teachers' interactions with middle and lower SES preschool boys and girls. *Journal of Educational Psychology*, 78, 495-498.

Rae, D. (1981). *Equalities.* Cambridge, MA: Harvard University Press.

Reinharz, S. (1986). The career controversy for women. *Educational Horizons*, 64, 136-139.

Robinson, J., Athanasious, R., and Head, K. (1969). Measures of occupational attitudes and occupational characteristics. Appendix A to *Measures of political attitudes*. Survey Research Center, Institute for Social Research.

Robinson, J., Shaver, P. and Wrightsman, L. (1991). *Measures of personality and social psychological attitudes*, 1. San Diego, CA: Academic Press Inc.

Rosenbaum, J. (1978). The structure of opportunity in school. *Social Forces*, 57, 236-256.

Rosenberg, M. (1981). The self-concept: Social product and social force. In M. Rosenberg and R. Turner (Eds.), *Social psychology: sociological perspectives* (pp. 593-624). New York: Basic Books, Inc.

Rosenberg, M. and L. Pearlin (1978). Social class and self-esteem among children and adults. *American Journal of Sociology*, 84, 53-77.

Rosenthal, R. and Jacobson, L. (1968). *Pygmalion in the classroom: Teacher expectation and pupils' intellectual development*. New York: Holt, Rinehart, and Winston.

Rossan, S. (1987). Identity and its development in adulthood. In Honess, T. and Yardley, K. (eds.). *Self and identity: Perspectives across the lifespan* (pp. 304-319). London: Routledge and Kegan Paul.

Ryan, J. (1996). "Even if you can't go home again, do it anyway!" *Race, Gender & Class*. Vol. 4, No. 1, 1996 (83-102).

Ryan, J., and Sackrey, C. (1996). *Strangers in paradise: Academics from the working class*. New York: University Press of America, Inc.

Ryan, R. (1991). The nature of the self in autonomy and relatedness. In Strauss, J. and Goethals, G., (eds.). *The self: Interdisciplinary approaches* (pp. 208-238). New York: Springer-Verlag.

Sandler, B., Silverberg, L., and Hall, R. (1996). *The chilly classroom climate: A guide to improve the education of women*. Washington, DC: The National Association for Women in Education.

Seidman, E. (1985). *In the words of the faculty: Perspectives on improving teaching and educational quality in community colleges.* San Francisco: Jossey-Bass Publishers.

Sennett, R. and Cobb, J. (1972). *The hidden injuries of class.* New York: Vintage Press.

Smith, L. (1994). Biographical method. In Denzin, N. and Lincoln, Y., Eds.. *Handbook of qualitative research* (pp. 286-305). Thousand Oaks, CA: Sage Publications.

Sokol, R. (1973). Status inconsistency: Specification of a theory (Doctoral dissertation, Columbia University, 1961). University Microfilms: Ann Arbor.

Steedman, C. (1995). Death of a good woman. In Blair, M., Holland, J., and Sheldon, S. (eds.). *Identity and diversity: Gender and the experience of education* (pp. 8-23). Clevedon, UK: Multilingual Matters Ltd.

Stewart, A. and Ostrove, J. (1993) Social class, social change, and gender: Working-class women at Radcliffe and after. In R. Under and J. Sanchez-Hucles (Eds.), *Psychology of Women Quarterly*, 17, 475-497. Cambridge, England: Cambridge University Press.

Stinchcombe, A. (1989). Education, exploitation, and class consciousness. In E. O. Wright (Ed.), *The debate on classes* (pp. 168-172). London, England: Verso.

Strauss, J. and Goethals, G., Eds. (1991). *The self: Interdisciplinary approaches.* New York: Springer-Verlag.

Stryker, S. (1987). Identity theory: Developments and extensions. In Yardley, K. and Honess, T., (eds.). *Self and identity: Psychosocial perspectives* (pp. 89-103). Chichester, UK: John Wiley and Sons.

Taylor, J., Gilligan, C., and Sullivan, A. (1995). *Between voice and silence: Women and girls, race and relationship.* Cambridge: Harvard University Press.

Thomas, S.C. (1996). A sociological perspective on contextualism. *Journal of Counseling and Development*, 74 (6), 529-536.

Tokarczyk, M., and Fay, E., Eds. (1993). *Working-class women in the academy: laborers in the knowledge factory.* Amherst, MA: University of Massachusetts Press.

Touchton, J. and Davis L. (1991). *Fact book on women in higher education.* New York: Macmillan Publishing Company.

Tsing, A.L. (1994). From the margins. *Cultural Anthropology,* 279-297.

Tsing, A.L.(1993). *In the realm of the diamond queen: Marginality in an out-of-the-way place.* Princeton, NJ: Princeton University Press.

Turner, R. (1987). Articulating self and social structure. In Yardley, K. and Honess, T., (eds.). *Self and identity: Psychosocial perspectives* (pp. 119-132). Chichester, UK: John Wiley and Sons.

Twombley, S.B. and Moore, K.M. (1991). Social origins of higher education administrators. *The Review of Higher Education,* 14, 485-510.

van Manen, M. (1990). *Researching lived experience.* London, Ontario, Canada: State University of New York Press.

West, M. (1995). Women faculty: Frozen in time. *Academe,* 26-29.

Yardley, K. and Honess, T., Eds. (1987). *Self and identity: Psychosocial perspectives.* Chichester, UK: John Wiley and Sons.

978-0-595-46942-0
0-595-46942-6

20123193R00107

Made in the USA
Lexington, KY
21 January 2013